Samuel French Acting Edition

The Founders

by Paul Green

Copyright © 1957 by Paul Green
All Rights Reserved

THE FOUNDERS is fully protected under the copyright laws of the United States of America, the British Commonwealth, including Canada, and all member countries of the Berne Convention for the Protection of Literary and Artistic Works, the Universal Copyright Convention, and/ or the World Trade Organization conforming to the Agreement on Trade Related Aspects of Intellectual Property Rights. All rights, including professional and amateur stage productions, recitation, lecturing, public reading, motion picture, radio broadcasting, television, online/digital production, and the rights of translation into foreign languages are strictly reserved.

ISBN 978-0-573-68014-4

www.concordtheatricals.com
www.concordtheatricals.co.uk

FOR PRODUCTION INQUIRIES

UNITED STATES AND CANADA
info@concordtheatricals.com
1-866-979-0447

UNITED KINGDOM AND EUROPE
licensing@concordtheatricals.co.uk
020-7054-7200

Each title is subject to availability from Concord Theatricals Corp., depending upon country of performance. Please be aware that *THE FOUNDERS* may not be licensed by Concord Theatricals Corp. in your territory. Professional and amateur producers should contact the nearest Concord Theatricals Corp. office or licensing partner to verify availability.

CAUTION: Professional and amateur producers are hereby warned that *THE FOUNDERS* is subject to a licensing fee. The purchase, renting, lending or use of this book does not constitute a license to perform this title(s), which license must be obtained from Concord Theatricals Corp. prior to any performance. Performance of this title(s) without a license is a violation of federal law and may subject the producer and/or presenter of such performances to civil penalties. Both amateurs and professionals considering a production are strongly advised to apply to the appropriate agent before starting rehearsals, advertising, or booking a theatre. A licensing fee must be paid whether the title(s) is presented for charity or gain and whether or not admission is charged. Professional/Stock licensing fees are quoted upon application to Concord Theatricals Corp.

This work is published by Samuel French, an imprint of Concord Theatricals Corp.

Please refer to page 211 for further copyright information.

For

ALLEN MATTHEWS, HOWARD SCAMMON, ROGER SHERMAN, SUE SHERMAN, MYRA KINCH, CARL FEHR, GENE STEEL, ADELINE MC CALL, AL HAAK, ANTHONY MANZI

—friends and co-workers in the making of this project.

AUTHOR'S NOTE: *Symphonic Drama*

As I worked at the drama, I felt again and again that I was involved in the same sort of enterprise as a composer driving forward his composition for some eighty or a hundred instruments. The whole body of the work must be kept propelling itself onward by means of the individual instrumentations which came forward to personal fulfillment, returned and gave place to others, and they in turn likewise. Motifs must be developed, thematic statements made and exploited, and a ferment of symphonic creativity be kept brewing to self-realization. And all to be sternly controlled by the architectonic power of the story line. Whatever failed to advance the story would not be used. For, after all, drama is storytelling. Of whatever sort, it is storytelling in action. Of course a little functional and lyrical decoration could be indulged in now and then. But only beauty spots, as it were, to be tinted in on the face of the whole.

And the *idée fixe*, say, as in a Beethoven or Berlioz symphony, the sensed and felt and inner form, call it even the melodic line, whether submerged or surfaced —must control matters.

The story line was a creature alive indeed. And even as the will-o'-the-wisp, he lived in and inhabited the scene. There the little creature enters from the street. He moves about the yard. The house calls to him. He enters there. He takes possession of a room for a while, and the human beings indwelling there are disturbed and thrown into fits even at his galvanic appearance— an appearance called up out of their own deep desires and activities, their clashing wills and urges in them-

AUTHOR'S NOTE

selves—just as the violins flutter and cry out in sweet stridency or joyful pain as the burden of the symphonic movement develops or comes to being in their vibrating and shaken bosoms.

I kept searching for a term of definition and interpretation to describe my play as I worked at it.

I found that in trying to express the inner lives and turmoilings of my characters I was having to call upon nearly all the available elements in modern theatrical art. And there were plenty of them. Folk song and poetry were needed here. Likewise the dance and pantomime and chorus voices. Even the mental speech of the grisly microphone and echo chamber could be used to get inside the soul life of some of my disturbed and vitalized people. Moments of horrification would call for masks. And ever there was the dynamic flow and modulation of light to accompany the human behavior at work. Light that would illuminate a volatile and advancing story point. And in that illumination the mind of the appreciator could read the message clear. The fabled fire in the Scriptures was like this light, the furnace fire in which the Hebrew children once stood all bright and glorified.

And always there was music—music!

"Music drama" didn't seem the right term for the play. "Ballad opera" it couldn't be. Nor "opera." "Festival play" was too loose and misnoming. "Lyric drama" lacked entirety. Finally "symphonic drama" seemed right. Yes, a "sounding-together" in the true meaning of the Greek word . . . It was nearer what I wanted than anything else. And so I adopted it and have continued to use it for other like plays I have written since.

From the author's *Dramatic Heritage*.
Permission of Samuel French, Inc.

CHARACTERS

(IN THE ORDER OF THEIR APPEARANCE)

Three Indian Warriors
Powhatan
Pocahontas
Rawhunt
Kocoum
Nicolas Scot
George Cassen
William Love
Edward Brinton
Reverend Robert Hunt
William Johnson
Edward Maria Wingfield
Christopher Newport
Bartholomew Gosnold
John Ratcliffe
George Kendall
John Martin
Gabriel Archer
George Percy
Thomas Studley
Eustis Clovill
Thomas Wotton
Nathaniel Powell
Jonas Profit, *the narrator*
John Laydon
John Dods
Thomas Barret
Thomas Webb
James Read
William White
William Garret
Richard Mutton
James Brumfield
Nat Peacock
Samuel Collier
Four or Five Sailors
Old Edward
Sir Austin Cooms
Pharaoh Perkins
Captain John Smith
Ananias Todkill
Sigismund Waller
Esau Crofts
Several Laboring Men
A Captive Indian Brave
Opecancanough
Several Indian Men and Women
Several Indian Maids
Two Indian Executioners
Jeffrey Abbot
Temperance Flowerdew
Barbara Blewett
Anne Laydon
Little Virginia Laydon
Thomas Forest
Lucy Forest
George Yeardley

CHARACTERS

- John Rolfe
- Several Soldiers and Sailors
- Sir Thomas Gates
- Sir George Somers
- William Strachey
- Francis West
- Thomas Savage
- Henry Spelman
- Reverend Richard Buck
- Martha Raynor
- Sir Thomas Dale
- Six or Eight Soldiers
- Captain Edward Brewster
- Ralph Hamor
- Polly Pace
- Tomasine Utley
- Cicely Jordan
- Isabella Proctor
- Goody Redhead
- Opachisco
- Patapsco
- Nantaquaus
- Joan Flinton
- Avis Glover
- Chloe Holland
- Hester Morrison
- Drusilla Wright
- Edward Gurganey
- William Spence
- Thomas Dowse
- Rufus Price
- Humphrey Green
- Joshua Swift
- Timothy Proctor
- Tony Brooks
- George Cotton
- Several Colonist Babies
- Little Thomas Rolfe
- Chanco
- Little Thomas Cooms
- Little John Cooms
- Two Colonist Women
- A Ship's Surgeon
- A Ship's Captain
- Captain William Powell
- John Polentine
- Samuel Sharpe
- Samuel Jordan
- Captain William Tucker
- William Capp

SCENES

PART ONE

SCENE 1 *The woods on Jamestown Island, May 1607.*
SCENE 2 *The fort at Jamestown, a few weeks later.*
SCENE 3 *The woods near the York River, sometime later.*
SCENE 4 *In and around the fort at Jamestown, sometime later.*
SCENE 5 *Aboard Sir Thomas Gates' ship* Deliverance *at Jamestown, June 1610.*
SCENE 6 *The woods near Jamestown, the next day.*
SCENE 7 *Interior of the fort at Jamestown, two days later.*

PART TWO

SCENE 1 *Interior of the fort at Jamestown, May 1611.*
SCENE 2 *In and around the fort at Jamestown, sometime later.*
SCENE 3 *The same, some months later.*
SCENE 4 *Interior of the fort at Jamestown, May 1616.*
SCENE 5 *Aboard the ship* George *at Gravesend, England, March 1617.*
SCENE 6 *In the woods near Jamestown, sometime later.*
SCENE 7 *In and around the fort at Jamestown, March 1622.*

PART ONE

Scene I

The audience is assembling in the amphitheatre for the play, and the big woodland center stage and lake beyond are gradually filling up with gloom. The stars come out, and a powerful and unseen organ begins the overture.

This overture is made up of sixteenth and seventeenth century English music mainly, with some Indian material mingled in. It is amplified and comes from different hidden sources on the center stage along the lake and from the wooded side stages of the surrounding forest. At first there is a cheery and challenging hunting horn call—a call with something of a zestful and exciting frosty morning feeling in it. It is repeated. Then follows the first half of the stately and grave old "Huguenot Battle Hymn" followed by a dynamic and somewhat sprightly colonist work song flooding in. This gives way to a murky upboiling of deep organ chords out of which emerges a faraway hollow Indian drumbeat. This fades and gives way to a mounting wailing of reed flutes and the slithery pebbly staccato of shaken gourds. The music seems to come from the right and pass on out at the left—a music expressive not only of a race of people with their passions, joy and pain, but of nature itself—of summer storms, of thunder and lightning, of hail and angry winds—all passing away finally into a quiet and soothing peace.

There is an instant of silence. Then a rat-tat-tat of organ snare drums begins far off at the right, above which rise the soaring mellow notes of English trumpets. The lights go down to half dim. The rat-tat-tat comes nearer, accompanied by the oncoming rhythmic beat of marching feet in the sound track —the marching feet of the English moving toward the new world, growing nearer and louder until the amphitheatre itself pulses with the sound. It moves across the stage from right to left and then fades to a final muffled trumpet call in the distance—and is heard no more.

The lights in the amphitheatre go down and out. The organ comes in again full and loud in a return to the latter half of the "Huguenot Battle Hymn" and concludes.

In the darkness of the shrouded forest around a single bird awakes and gives his saluting cheerful note to the now oncoming dawn. Another bird answers and then others—a growing din of whistling, chirpings and flutings rising from the vast woods. The gray light of morning begins to tinge the tops of the trees on the farther shore of the pearly, mirrored lake, and stray wisps of mist rise from the water and drift off in the upper air in little lazy swirls. The light increases on the

THE FOUNDERS

lake and trees as the wilderness repeats its immemorial awakening to the gladness of a May morning. The symphony of birdsong grows in volume. The first beams of the sun touch the tops of the distant trees, and at the same instant a great drum in the forest is struck a mighty reverberating blow.

The huge drum now begins a slow methodical beat—boom—boom—boom—the voiced heartbeat of the wilderness, never any slower, never any faster—boom—boom—boom— powerful, monstrous, and ominous.

Two half-crouching INDIAN WARRIORS *creep down out of the woods at the right and move toward the lake, peering ahead, watching and wary, carrying their bows in their hands, their tattooed half-naked bodies glistening with sweat, their heads and shoulders reddened with war paint, their faces blackened with oiled soot and marked with white and vermilion streakings. A* THIRD WARRIOR *similarly armed and painted hurries down from the woods at the right and joins the other two. The three stop, slip toward the left rear, and stare off. They send out high-pitched signal whistles—"pfu-ee-ee!" Other whistles answer them likewise from different parts of the forest. The wilderness is growing conscious of some disturbance, some coming enemy as it were that troubles it. The birdsong suddenly ceases. The drum lightly increases its volume, and the* INDIANS *crouch behind a fringe of bushes and carefully raise their heads gazing out across the lake.*

In a sort of halo of light a ship like a great white bird appears there on the water moving diagonally upstream from right to left. As it appears, the drum gives a spurt of sound in reaction to the sight and continues more loudly. The INDIANS *spring up and stand motionless.*

There is a gap of silence in the drumbeat. From the ship comes the far-off sound of an English trumpet giving a salute to the land, followed by a distant chorus of men's voices singing a hymn in a harmony of indistinguishable words. The INDIANS *turn and move toward the forest edge at the left, stop again and look back. The light on the ship dies out and comes up at the left. There as if on an overlook in the forest the great Indian chieftain* POWHATAN *appears, coming out of the leafy shadows at the rear and staring off toward the river. A loud flurry in the drum announces him. With him are his little daughter* POCAHONTAS *or* MATOAKA *as she is often called and his dwarfish medicine man, the huskanawed cockarouse,* RAWHUNT.

POWHATAN *is a tall grizzled old man about seventy years old, bony and loose-framed, and carrying a long feather-topped staff in his hand. A big flat copper plate is fastened to one side of his head for ornament, and two long eagle feathers are stuck in a leather circlet around his head, hanging over and down like two horns. He wears a loincloth and moccasins, and his great shoulders are draped in a coonskin coat with tasseled tails.*

THE FOUNDERS

His visage is grim and wrinkled and marked with a scattering of long white hairs for a beard. William Strachey, one of the early colony historians, described him as "a goodly old man and not yet shrinking, though well-beaten with many cold winters . . . with gray hairs but plain and thin hanging on his broad shoulders . . . He hath been a strong and able savage, sinewy, and of a daring spirit, vigilant, ambitious, subtle."

POCAHONTAS *is a spirited, petted young girl about thirteen years old, a little below medium height and wearing the dress becoming to an Indian maid who has just passed from the frank innocence of childhood into clothed womanhood. Her short deerskin kirtle is bright-patterned with embroidered flower and animal designs, and her sleeveless little white-feathered jacket only partly conceals her swelling breasts. Her somewhat oval face is expressive of modesty and girlish frankness, and her coal-black eyes are large and serene, though for the moment sparkling with excitement. Her raven hair is pulled well back from her low forehead to hang down in a long tail behind her back and tied by a woodbine and set with a copper ornament. She is bare-legged but wears moccasins.*

RAWHUNT *is an outlandish elderly character, emaciated and runtish, wearing a short tattered rabbit-skin cloak made like a woman's petticoat and fastened about his neck and coming down only to his middle. For modesty's sake he wears an otter-skin girdle with the tail tied between his legs. His head is shaved except for a middle roach of hair like a rooster's comb and painted red as a sapsucker's. His face is blackened with soot and his eyes circled by white rings. A great eagle claw protrudes through a hole in the lobe of each ear, and from his neck is suspended the dried hand of some former murdered enemy. For headgear he wears a coronet of feathers from which some dozen or more stuffed snake skins hang down in grisly jiggling tassels over his shoulders. He carries a gourd rattle in each hand.*

The THREE WARRIORS *now bow in obeisance before* POWHATAN, *then get behind him as if seeking the protection of his power.* POCAHONTAS *steps forward and stands by her father. She gazes off with wonder and childish delight. She points and looks joyously up at the old chief. His grim visage causes the smile to die from her face.*

RAWHUNT *springs suddenly out and shakes his rattles in the air before him as if warding off some evil influence that threatens them. The unseen drum continues its beating.* KOCOUM, *a lithe and sinewed young Indian brave of eighteen or nineteen, comes in from the shadows and stands close to* POCAHONTAS. *He is naked save for his loincloth and is unpainted. He takes her hand possessively and stares off. She moves farther out on the overlook straining her gaze toward the water. She speaks in an awed voice saying that the men*

THE FOUNDERS 9

on the great winged ship are like gods maybe, come from the clouds above.

POCAHONTAS. Kewosowok mamaum!

[POWHATAN *makes no answer, standing there a moment motionless and lordly. Then abruptly he barks a command at the* WARRIORS *in his great phlegmy voice, bidding them to summons the people.*]

POWHATAN. Ireh assuminge!

[*The* WARRIORS *throw up their right hands in acknowledgment of his order, answering that they obey their mighty chief.*

WARRIORS. [*In unison.*] Cuppeh, Mamanatowick!

[*They dart away into the forest.* POWHATAN *draws his cloak about him, puts his fist against the knob of his chin in thought and then turns back into the shadows,* RAWHUNT *going before and shaking his rattles.* KOCOUM *follows,* POCAHONTAS *remaining behind. The great volume of the drum which has built rapidly to a climax now begins to die down.* POCAHONTAS *stands gazing off, the light focusing on her. The drum continues to die. Finally it is silent. From the forest* POWHATAN *calls out roughly for her to hurry along.*]

POWHATAN. Camerowath, Matoaka!

[KOCOUM *re-enters to fetch her, telling her to come quickly.*]

KOCOUM. Pocahontas, pyak, pyak!

[*He takes her by the hand to lead her off. She jerks away from him, and then skips gaily off after her father.*

KOCOUM *trots along behind. The scene fades out. Again there is a moment of silence. From the darkness toward the lake a trumpet blows a high salute. A burst of men's lusty singing begins in the distance, accompanied by the rat-tat-tat of a snare drum. The light comes up full on the center stage revealing a cleared grassy place on the bank of the James River. Over at the left rear is a little hillock with wild flowers growing on it. A procession of colonists is coming up the incline at the right rear as if from a ship anchored off scene. The men are singing strongly as they come. Leading the way are* NICOLAS SCOT, *18, with his drum and* GEORGE CASSEN, *17, with his trumpet. Two flagbearers—*WILLIAM LOVE, *21, and* EDWARD BRINTON, *19—are behind them.* LOVE *carries the flag of Britain and* BRINTON *the flag of the English church. Next come the colony minister, the Reverend Master* ROBERT HUNT, *35, and* WILLIAM JOHNSON, *22.* MR. HUNT *is dressed in his monkish gown, and apparels proper for the occasion, with a Bible clasped against his breast, and* JOHNSON *is holding a tall cross aloft. Behind them is* EDWARD MARIA WINGFIELD, *47, the president of the colony, with his staff of office in his hand. Following him come the members of His Majesty's Council for the First Colony in Virginia—Captains* CHRISTOPHER NEWPORT, *42;* BARTHOLOMEW GOSNOLD, *43;* JOHN RATCLIFFE, *30;* GEORGE KENDALL, *37; and* JOHN MARTIN, *45.* MARTIN *holds a little box about a foot square in his arms. Next are a number of gentlemen—*GABRIEL ARCHER, *31;* GEORGE PERCY, *27;* THOMAS STUDLEY, *35;* EUSTIS CLOVILL, *30; and* THOMAS WOTTON, *40, the last the colony surgeon. Some of these men are bearded, some cleanshaven, and their dress is brilliant and varied as becomes their place in the society of the time. After*

THE FOUNDERS

them enters CAPTAIN NATHANIEL POWELL, *28, a cleancut young man in armor and belted sword, commanding a group of soldiers armed with muskets. Among the soldiers are* JONAS PROFIT, *25;* JOHN LAYDON, *27;* JOHN DODS, *21;* THOMAS BARRET, *21;* THOMAS WEBB, *22;* JAMES READ, *24;* WILLIAM WHITE, *26; and* WILLIAM GARRET, *19. Clustering along with the soldiers are four boys 10 to 12 years of age*—RICHARD MUTTON, JAMES BRUMFIELD, NAT PEACOCK *and* SAMUEL COLLIER. *Last in the line are four or five sailors and with them a gnarled and ancient fellow of indeterminate age known as* OLD EDWARD *who drags a shovel along in his hand. The colonists march across the scene from the right rear to the left front, turn again toward the left rear and gather in a circle where* PRESIDENT WINGFIELD *has stopped and planted his staff against the ground. The assembly now wings out from the president. The singing has continued—the powerful and marching "Huguenot Battle Hymn" which we first heard from the ship on the river.*]

COLONISTS. [*Joyously, vibrantly.*]
>   To God the earth doth appertain,
>   The world also is his domain
>   And all that therein dwelleth.
>   For he hath founded it full fast
>   And 'stablished it t'abide and last,
>   And it his mercy filleth.
>   Wherefore let joyful voices ring,
>   His name in loud hosannas sing,
>   All praise to him be given.
>   The seraphim and hosts on high
>   Adore his grace and majesty,
>   Ruler of earth and heaven.

THE FOUNDERS

[PRESIDENT WINGFIELD *lifts his staff as the singing ends, and* HUNT *steps to his side.* JOHNSON *sets the tall cross down and holds it leaningly in the scene.* LOVE *lowers the flag of Britain a bit subservient to it.*]

WINGFIELD. [*Loudly.*] Here on the thirteenth day of May in the year of our Lord sixteen hundred and seven we the founders of the first colony of Virginia do take possession of this island—in the name of our most sovereign king, James the First, by the grace of God of England, Ireland, Scotland, Wales—and now Virginia!

[SCOT *gives a roll of his drum, and* CASSEN *lifts his trumpet and blows a saluting blast.*]

COLONISTS. [*With a great shout.*] Eigh-yah! In the name of his majesty the king!

WINGFIELD. We lift our flag over this new and vast empire that stretches to the southern sea.

[LOVE *waves the flag back and forth.*]

And as Englishmen we shall defend it against Spain, the pope and all enemies whatsoever with our arms, our honor and our blood.

COLONISTS. [*Again with a great shout.*] Yea, we shall!

WINGFIELD AND COLONISTS. So help us God!

WINGFIELD. On April twenty-six we planted our cross at the new land of Cape Henry. Here on this island we again affirm our dominion.

[*He gestures to* OLD EDWARD *who moves over to the hillock with his shovel and begins the pantomime of digging.* JOHNSON *lifts the cross forward, and* HUNT *holds up his hands.*]

HUNT. We now break ground for this our church and set once more toward heaven the emblem of our true religion, of God's mercy and good favor upon us.

MARTIN. [*Calling out.*] And on this site we build our habitations.

COLONISTS. Amen.

[SIR AUSTIN COOMS, *40, blooming like a gaudy flower, enters at the left rear. He is a most special and finicky gentleman of ribbons, perfume and laces, a nonpareil of foppishness, and is accompanied by his manservant* PHARAOH PERKINS, *30, who holds a pink and feminine parasol over his master to protect him from the heat. The two of them stop at the edge of the assemblage. A few people notice them, and snickers break out here and there.* SIR AUSTIN *ignores this rabble. The cross is now set up, and* OLD EDWARD *tamps the dirt around it with the handle of his shovel.*]

HUNT. [*Lifting his Bible.*] Verily the Lord hath said, "I will make thee a great nation and will bless thee and make thy name great."

COLONISTS. [*Intoning.*] Blessed be the name of the Lord!

[CAPTAIN JOHN SMITH *comes stamping his way in from the right rear. He is about 28 years old, a stiff stocky figure of a man, bareheaded, bearded and in armor. His wrists are manacled in heavy irons.* ANANIAS TODKILL, *25, a soldier with a musket slung over his shoulder, is trying to pull him back.*]

TODKILL. Nay, Captain Smith, nay!

WINGFIELD. Why this unseemly disturbance, Captain John Smith, and thee in irons?

SMITH. [*Loudly.*] From the deck of the ship there, Master President, I could see thee here with no care for the safety of this gathering. I came to warn you.

TODKILL. [*Piteously.*] I pleaded, sir, but he would not hearken.

[*A murmur rises among the* COLONISTS. *There is obviously some show of sympathy for* SMITH.]

WINGFIELD. [*Sternly to* SMITH.] For thy conspiring on the high seas just judgement was passed upon thee. Two days more of thy servitude remain.

SMITH. Conspiring! [*Fiercely.*] When I saw mutiny about to break I conspired to put it down with a strong hand. Naught else.

WINGFIELD. And there was no mutiny for all thy plotting, thanks be unto God.

SMITH. Yea, for we sighted land in time to calm all rebellious souls. And now I charge thee to set a guard to protect this assembly.

WINGFIELD. [*Angrily.*] When I as president say so.

SMITH. Who knows but the savages may be skulking in the reeds about this spot even as at Cape Henry.

WINGFIELD. We come in peace with no show of arms to the naturals. 'Tis the terms of our company's charter.

RATCLIFFE AND KENDALL. Aye.

SMITH. [*Harshly.*] But the charter was writ three thousand miles away in England. We are here in the wilderness of Virginia.

WINGFIELD. Silence! I command thee back to thy prison

quarters aboard ship. Soldier White, Soldier Read! [*Gesturing.*] Take him away.

[*The* TWO SOLDIERS *step quickly up to* SMITH *with their muskets at the ready.* SMITH *glares about him.* TODKILL *takes hold of his arm and with* WHITE *and* READ *marches him back the way he came. He kicks the earth moodily as he goes. The murmur among the colonists dies out, and the ceremony is resumed.*]

HUNT. Verily God hath said, "They that go down to the sea in ships, that do business in great waters, these see the works of the Lord and his wonders in the deep. He maketh the storm a calm, so that the waves thereof are still. Then are they glad because they be quiet, so he bringeth them unto their desired haven." Name this city!

WINGFIELD AND COUNCILORS. [*In loud unison.*] James his town in Virginia—in honor of our king!

WINGFIELD. Let the English seed be brought forward.

[MARTIN *hands forward the small square wooden box which* HUNT *takes.*]

HUNT. The Lord's blessing be upon these seeds which we have brought to plant here in this new world. And as they spring from the earth so may our works flourish and grow green forevermore.

COLONISTS. May it be so.

[HUNT *now holds the box up high as if making an offering of it to God, then returns it to* MARTIN. *He raises his face in fervent prayer and the people bow their heads.*]

HUNT. Almighty and everlasting God, bless our king and prince of England. And bless the Virginia Company in London—each member thereof—who have begot this enterprise and with their treasure and labor sent it forth. Bless our sweet native country from which our duty hath called us.

PEOPLE. We beseech it.

HUNT. We lift our hearts to thee in thanksgiving—for thou has guided our three ships each and several safely over the raging seas to this our new home. Thou hast preserved us from the immovable rocks and the immutable winds, the overflowing waters and swallowing sands—from spoiling Spanish pirates and tempestuous storms—with only a few inches of plank between us and sudden death. Even as thou hast saved us aforetime so thou wilt continue to keep us from harm—

[*At this instant there is a loud swish of an arrow through the air from the depths of the woods at the right and the following plop as it hits its mark.* EUSTIS CLOVILL *throws up his hands with a scream and spins about clutching madly at the long shaft that has pierced him through.*]

VOICES. [*Wildly.*] Indians! The Indians are upon us!

MARTIN. Look to Master Clovill!

[*There is a turmoil on the center stage.* MARTIN *and* HUNT *kneel down by the dying man as he writhes and claws on the ground.* CASSEN *sounds an alarm on his trumpet.* WINGFIELD *and the* COUNCILORS *move about among the people trying to quiet them as they stare about at the encircling forest with horror in their faces. Some of the* BOYS *begin to sob and cling to the* COLONISTS *near them.* NEWPORT *shouts out.*]

NEWPORT. To your places, men! On guard!

THE FOUNDERS

WINGFIELD. Captain Powell, put soldiers around!

[CAPTAIN POWELL *is seen sending* SOLDIERS *to the rear and right and left.*]

POWELL. You, Dods, Laydon—up to the right there! [DODS *and* LAYDON *run up into the woods at the right.*] Jonas Profit, stand watch there at the edge of the forest! [JONAS PROFIT *goes up to the left.*]

MARTIN. We should fortify ourselves at once against the savages. They may attack us in force.

WINGFIELD AND OTHERS. Aye.

NEWPORT. [*To the* SAILORS.] Unload the cannon from the ships!

[*The* SAILORS *hurry out at the right rear.*]

WINGFIELD. Bear the body aboard where it will be prepared for Christian burial. Come away!

[*The body is taken up and borne aloft. The drum begins to beat, and the assemblage moves raggle-taggledly out at the right rear as the organ plays the "Huguenot Battle Hymn" like a dead march. The light dims down somewhat on the scene, holds an instant on the cross and the flag and the* SOLDIERS *standing guardingly around them, then blacks out. The organ surges in with a reprise of the last bars of the hymn and dies. A spotlight comes suddenly up on* JONAS PROFIT *standing motionless at the left in the edge of the forest. He is a strong, able-bodied young fellow, though somewhat lame in one foot. His back is toward us. A moment he stands so and then turns and comes down the incline a step or two. Holding his musket carelessly in the crook of his arm, he looks out across the amphitheatre at the audience.*]

JONAS. [*In an easy straight-forward manner.*] And that's how we begun our settlement here in Jamestown —begun it as you saw with death from the Indians and an argument of tongues—all to happen again and again in the days to come whilst the simple fellows like me looked on—until later when with Master John Rolfe and Captain Yeardley and others we started taking a hand in these matters. But that's to come. Proud and willful our leaders were like true Englishmen and each with a mind of his own. If we'd a-knowed the years of trials and tribulations that lay ahead of us here at Jamestown that winter day we sailed from the Downs of England with singing in our mouths—Lord a-mercy, every mother's son of us would druther had the root of his tongue cut from the gullet of his throat than set foot in the ships that brung us here. [*Taking another step down the incline.*] I was here—I saw the things that happened in this settlement, the suffering and the struggle, the weak hearts and the brave ones—and it changed the thinking of a lot of us. It changed me. And I'll tell ye about it all now and then as time goes by. [*Clearing his throat.*] My name is Profit—Jonas Profit—not a Bible prophet that can see the truth way off in a cloud, nor a man to skim off a handful of yellow ducats for profit here below. I can hardly read—but I know how to spell my name, P-r-o-f-i-t. My mammy taught me my letters ere they shut her away witless in Bedlam town. [*Gesturing toward the right with his free hand.*] I am listed in the great colony book there for a fisherman and a soldier. I was hungry and homeless like so many others on the streets of London with no calling or trade and had to put down something to get here to this new land. [*Taking another step.*] They said there'd be a chance here for fellows such as me. Yea, when the settlement was fixed and founded strong and I had served my time, they said, and they had gathered gold and silver from the rocks in the hills, there'd be a bit of it for me maybe, and a piece of farm land too— me, whose folks from the time of old Richard Lionheart hisself had never more than six foot of earth and that for their own funeral shrouding. I would be honored likewise for serving my king and country and have my rights as an Englishman, they said. [*With a touch of wryness.*] My rights, whatever they are. It's all in the charter, though, that the great king give to the Virginia Company of lords and leaders for the colony here. Captain Smith read it out for us one night on the long voyage coming over, the whilst the fearful water-witches were crying round the ship. A righthearted man Captain Smith, but with a mouth too big and quick-speaking for his own good, no doubt, and always projecking and jumping ahead till he got blowed up by gunpowder in an accident one day and went away half-dead to England forevermore.

[*From the darkness of the center stage* SERGEANT TODKILL *is heard calling.*]

TODKILL. Jonas Profit! Jonas Profit!

JONAS. Aye, they're all working fierce now building the fort and our habitations. And Sergeant Todkill is calling me. And well it is so. When that arrow went through Master Eustis Clovill the day we landed it taught us a lot of things. It taught us not to trust the Indians and especially old chief Powhatan and his younger brother, Chief Opecancanough. They hated us from the first, said we'd come to take the Indians' land —[*Chuckling.*] And so we had, I reckon. [*He moves a step more down the incline and then stops.*] But the

Princess Pocahontas was always our friend as it turned out, strange but she was, and ever trying to keep peace betwixt us and her people. She loved us. And her father —dark and sulling old chief he was—he dearly loved her. She had great power over him and her people, and more than once she stood between us and grisly creeping death.

TODKILL. Jonas Profit!

JONAS. Coming, Sergeant, coming.

[GARRET, *weary and sweat-stained, comes up from the shadows and mounts guard, standing bent over on his musket, his back to the audience.* JONAS *goes on down toward the center stage. The light fades out, and from the darkness a medley of sounds breaks out—sawing, hammering, chopping of axes and voices raised in shouts and orders.*]

VOICES. [*Led by* TODKILL.] Swing them mattocks! Hup —hup—hup! Raise that palisado. Heave up, heave up, hup!

[*A labor song begins as the light rises on the center stage.*]

Scene II

The interior of the partially built fort. A pother of lusty labor and singing is going on. The scene is lighted in such a way that spots of activity are picked out in contrast to the shadowed part of the stage. Two cannon have been placed at the right and left center, pointing outward toward the surrounding wilderness. At the right front is the end of the storehouse projecting in. It is pretty much finished and JOHN LAYDON *is on the roof doing the last of the thatching, pulling a thong of oak splints through and fastening it. A ladder is leaning against the building.* JOHN DODS *is working at the final fitting of the lock on the door. At the right rear a short strip of palisades has been set and three or four men are raising other pointed logs to fit into it. Revealed in a deluge of burning sunlight at the center rear is a line of some five or six men stripped to the waist and digging the palisade ditch forward, lifting their picks and mattocks and driving them down, their bodies glistening with sweat. Among them are* BARRET, READ *and* OLD EDWARD. *Three or four shovelers are working behind them.* TODKILL *is in charge there. Over at the left* LOVE *and* BRINTON *are busy at the framework of a*

cabin. At the center rear JOHNSON *and* WHITE
*are sawing off the end of a palisade log while
the two boys,* DICK MUTTON *and* JIM BRUM-
FIELD, *hold it down in the crotched saw
frame. Men carrying bucket yokes over their
shoulders loaded with daubing mortar pass
along from right to left toward the church
which is being built off scene at the left and
from whence now and then sounds of hammering, mauling, chopping and shouted commands "Ease it to the right!"—"Lower it in
the socket!"—"Drive the pinion home!" are
heard. Along the river bank at the rear beyond the palisades a* SOLDIER *passes now and
then on his post of guard.* JONAS *walks into
the scene, and laying aside his musket, begins helping raise the heavy palisades. Three
fancy-dressed* GENTLEMEN *are seen strolling
about and conversing idly with one another,
pointing with their canes and watching the
splurge of work with cool and incidental
curiosity. The first of these is the foppish*
AUSTIN COOMS *without his parasol, and the
other two, men of middle age, are* SIGISMUND
WALLER *and* ESAU CROFTS. *The picks fall, the
hammers ring, and the sawyers keep up their
whee-ah, whee-ah, all pretty much in rhythm
to the song.*

WORKERS. [*Led by* TODKILL.]

Heave ho, ye men of England, stout of heart and hand,
We toil for God and king and so subdue the land.
Fast in the wilderness we build our hearth and home,
Far over ocean's mighty main and salt-sea foam.

THE FOUNDERS

—Through heat and rain and cold we carry on
To cease not till this blessed work be done.

All in the merry month of May we landed here.
To work, to work, the captain said in accents clear—
With axe and adze and hoe, the hammer and the maul!
Yea, swing them with a right good will and let them fall!
—Through heat and rain and cold we carry on,
To cease not till this blessed work be done.

[*They go on whistling the song.* CAPTAINS MARTIN *and* POWELL *come rapidly in at the left rear. They look about them overseeing things.* MARTIN *feels one of the palisadoes for steadiness and gestures his approval to the men. He and* POWELL *come on through the scene toward the storehouse at the right. The whistling stops but the pantomime of work goes on.*]

MARTIN. How goes the storehouse, John Laydon?

LAYDON. [*Saluting as he descends the ladder.*] Aye, Captain Martin, just finishing—and as stout a building as ever was made in England.

MARTIN. Good, good.

DODS. And this here door—a battering ram couldn't bust it down.

MARTIN. Most excellent.

LAYDON. If you'll acquaint the president, sir. He wanted to know when it was done.

MARTIN. He is having his after-dinner wine under the oak tree there. [*He gestures slightly toward the left, examines the door and is satisfied.*] Keep oversight, Captain Powell, I will see Captain Newport about the supplies.

[*He goes out at the right.* POWELL *turns hurriedly to the rear, bumping into* AUSTIN COOMS *and jostling him out of the way.*]

POWELL. A world of pardons, Sir Austin Cooms.

[AUSTIN *is outdone. He raises his cane threateningly, then hides it behind him as* POWELL *looks back. Some of the men laugh.* AUSTIN *glares over at them.*]

AUSTIN. [*Angrily.*] Back in England the common sort dared not laugh at their betters.

TODKILL. [*Merrily.*] But here they do already.

POWELL. Yea, when they will not work.

AUSTIN. [*Scandalized.*] Work! A gentleman work!

TODKILL. [*A little irritatedly.*] Ye may come to it yet, Sir Austin!

[AUSTIN *and his companions turn toward the left.* PHARAOH *comes trotting in from the right with a parasol.*]

PHARAOH. I seed you here in the heat, Master, and feared a distemper for ye. [*He opens the parasol and hands it to* AUSTIN *who holds it above his head.*]

AUSTIN. Thou art a faithful servant to me, Pharaoh. [*Staring at* PHARAOH's *hands.*] Ah, thy hands show the labor is hard they give ye to do.

PHARAOH. Aye, sir, stirring in that mommick and mixtry of daubing mud all day.

AUSTIN. We must bear it betimes, lad.

PHARAOH. We must, sir. But at night I'll ever tend ye faithful.

AUSTIN. Yea, with thy fan and vinegar cloth. 'Fore heaven, the Virginia mosqueeters puncture me like a sieve and let my blood. But we shall soon fare with the governor president and his men into the hills for gold and this be ended.

PHARAOH. Yes, sir, when the fort is built and we be safe from the fearsome red man.

[*He goes back the way he came.* AUSTIN *and his companions move away to the left.* OLD EDWARD *at the rear suddenly drops his mattock and clasping the back of his trousers with his hand, charges out at the right.*]

BARRET. [*As he lifts his mattock for digging.*] Yea, Old Edward trots to the bushes!

READ. Every five minute—to 'scape work.

BARRET. Says the bloody flux has seized him.

READ. Then he eats less, and we should have his food.

TODKILL. [*Reprimandingly.*] Speak not of food, 'tis two hours more ere the cooks call.

[*The work goes on. A shaft of burning light comes up across the front and several men enter along from the right stiff-legged, two by two, reared back, fiercely straining at their handspikes as they carry a big shaped timber onward.* WEBB, *one of the handspike men, stumbles and falls from weakness. The others slide the weighty beam on down to the ground with a groan.* POWELL *hurries forward to the fallen man and hauls him to his feet.*]

POWELL. Now none of that, Thomas Webb! To work!

[*He releases* WEBB, *who topples moaning to the ground again, his hands pressed against his stomach.*]

BARRET. [*Calling out.*] He's not able to eat for two days, Captain Powell.

POWELL. [*Relenting.*] Well, help him away.

[BARRET *and* READ *help the sick man off at the right and return.* POWELL *looks around for one to fill in. He gestures to* BRINTON *who comes over and takes his place at the spike. The heavy beam is raised with straining again and carried on off to the left. The work keeps going. A high Indian yell is heard in the woods up at the right. A number of workers drop their tools and seize their muskets which are lying handy.* CAPTAIN SMITH *and two armed* SOLDIERS *come marching down the incline, driving a captive* INDIAN BRAVE *along with his hands tied behind him.* SMITH *is coatless, his sleeves rolled up.*]

SMITH. [*Shoving the* INDIAN *forward as they enter.*] Get on there, ye varlet!

INDIAN. [*Shrieking his imprecation that the white men are devils.*] Tassentassis kiwasa!

POWELL. How now, Captain Smith?

[JOHN RATCLIFFE *enters from the left.*]

SMITH. Another thieving Indian. They creep up in the woods and spy on us. We seized him in the pocosin whilst cutting our thatching reeds. [*The* INDIAN *lets out his yell again.*]

INDIAN. Neire—Matoaka—Matoaka nim!

SMITH. He claims Pocahontas for his friend. But he lies. 'Tis one of Opecancanough's men. I know his markings.

RATCLIFFE. Best take him to Master Wingfield.

SMITH. I doubt not I will flog him—or bore his tongue with a red-hot iron. [*Loudly.*] Back to your work, men, we are well guarded around!

[*The struggling* INDIAN *is marched off at the left. The men put aside their muskets and return to work. Some of the* COLONISTS *re-enter from the left with their empty yokes and buckets, cross the scene and go on out the way they came.* HUNT *comes in from the right.*]

RATCLIFFE. How is it with Captain Gosnold, Master Hunt?

HUNT. Surgeon Wotton has bled and cupped him, Master Ratcliffe, and says he will mend.

RATCLIFFE. I pray so.

HUNT. [*Pushing his hand vaguely across his forehead.*] I understand not these strange afflictions that are seizing our men, the fevers and the swellings, the fluxes.

RATCLIFFE. It is the new climate. Soon we will be seasoned to it.

HUNT. God grant it. [*Dropping his hand quickly.*] And he will.

RATCLIFFE. Yea.

[*In the distance at the left the sound of blows is heard.* HUNT *puts his fingers in his ears to keep out the sound.*]

LAYDON. [*Grimly.*] Captain Smith is teaching that Indian a lesson with the cudgel.

DODS. I doubt you can teach an Indian anything.

[HUNT *goes on to the left meeting* PRESIDENT WING-

FIELD, PERCY *and* KENDALL. *They lift their hands in greeting as they pass and look about the scene with satisfaction. The boy,* SAMUEL COLLIER, *enters behind the president, with a pipe and a coal of fire in it.*]

SAMUEL. Your pipe, sir. [*He hands it to* WINGFIELD.]

WINGFIELD. [*To* POWELL.] Take some of your men, Captain Powell. The roof-tree for the church is ready for raising.

POWELL. [*Saluting.*] Yes, sir. And, Profit, you see to the diggers.

[POWELL *and* TODKILL *go about choosing the men at the right and left,* LAYDON *and* DODS *among them, and they follow them off, leaving the* DIGGERS *only at their work with* JONAS *in charge.* WINGFIELD *lifts his pipe and takes a draw.*]

WINGFIELD. What in mercy's name is this! It scorches my tongue like fire.

SAMUEL. Indian tobacco, sir. Pocahontas brought it from her father.

WINGFIELD. [*To* SAMUEL.] Take it away. If old Powhatan's heart be no kinder than this vile stuff, then 'tis black as the pit itself.

[*The boy takes the pipe away.* MARTIN *comes stepping rapidly in at the right, followed by a* SAILOR *with a bag on his shoulder. He gestures to the* SAILOR *to set the bag down. He does so and returns the way he came.* MARTIN *is upset. He strides up to* WINGFIELD *and opens his clenched hand.*]

MARTIN. What is that, Master President?

WINGFIELD. I know not, Captain Martin.

MARTIN. Biscuit bread from the ship's hold.

[RATCLIFFE *steps quickly forward and takes the biscuit from* MARTIN's *hand.*]

RATCLIFFE. [*In a shocked voice.*] And spoiled!

[SMITH *comes in at the left.*]

WINGFIELD. What's that? What say ye?

[SMITH *notices the concern of the group, hurries over to the bag and pulls out some blackened putrid bread.*]

SMITH. Our biscuit, President Wingfield.

[*He holds it up. The* COUNCILORS *crowd around him. More of the bread is brought out from the bag. The reaction of the* COUNCILORS *shows the seriousness of the news. The light has dimmed down somewhat on the* DIGGERS *at the rear as they carry on their pantomime of work. It remains on* WINGFIELD *and his group.*]

RATCLIFFE. Is much of it spoiled?

MARTIN. All, Master Ratcliffe. Black with mold.

WINGFIELD. Nay, I do not believe it!

MARTIN. Rotten in the ship's hold.

SMITH. [*Hotly to* WINGFIELD.] As I told you it would be. A week ago I urged you to have it up and into the wholesome air.

WINGFIELD. There was no room, Captain Smith.

SMITH. Room a-plenty—with sailcloth over it and guards to protect it. But you would not.

WINGFIELD. Nay, I would not at thy bidding.

SMITH. Bidding! Good reason was bidding enough.

RATCLIFFE. Gentlemen!

WINGFIELD. Ah, Captain Newport. [NEWPORT *comes in at the right.*] What is this mad tale?

NEWPORT. It is true. John Martin and I examined the biscuit. All is spoilt.

MARTIN. And the rats have eaten much of our grain.

[*The* COUNCILORS *look at one another.*]

KENDALL. Then our bread supply is fearfully scant.

PERCY. What is to be done?

SMITH. The council should first elect a new president.

WINGFIELD. [*His hand on his sword.*] You were once placed in chains for a mutinous tongue, Captain Smith. Look to it lest the next time you receive your proper due on the gallows tree.

SMITH. [*His hand on his sword likewise.*] And I defy thy authority.

MARTIN, RATCLIFFE AND OTHERS. Nay, nay.

SMITH. Are we leaders or fools! We have come here to found this colony, and from the beginning all has been mismanaged—bickerings and blindness! Who is to blame? Who but the one in authority—the president himself? [*Bitingly.*] And certain members of his council.

WINGFIELD. Save thy speech, Captain Smith, or I'll call the guard and slap thee in the ship's hold as a prisoner to be taken away to England.

THE FOUNDERS

[SMITH *draws his sword in a flash.* MARTIN *and others step between the two men.*]

MARTIN. Gentlemen, gentlemen, cease these quarrels. [*They quiet the two, and* MARTIN *turns to* NEWPORT.] What do you advise, Captain Newport?

NEWPORT. That I take the few bundles of sassafras roots and earth ore we have collected and sail home to the Company for supplies. [*They nod.*] I will finish unloading, and be ready to leave at the first fair wind.

[*He salutes and goes out at the right.* OLD EDWARD *reenters at the rear and takes his place among the* DIGGERS.]

RATCLIFFE. [*Hopefully.*] The Virginia Company will be sending out Sir Thomas Gates and a fleet of ships ere long.

KENDALL. And soon our corn crop will be harvested.

SMITH. Aye, in sixty days.

MARTIN. And a poor crop it will be at this late planting.

SMITH. [*Announcingly.*] The Indians must help us.

PERCY AND KENDALL. The Indians!

SMITH. Powhatan's people. But yesterday his daughter Pocahontas brought greetings of friendship from him. I will take trinkets and go trade with him. Give me a few men and the barge and I promise to bring it loaded with corn.

KENDALL. But what of Opecancanough?

PERCY. Powhatan is lord over his brother.

RATCLIFFE. [*To* SMITH.] You have just flogged one of his men.

SMITH. I fear not Opecancanough nor Powhatan.

WINGFIELD. Captain Smith fears no man.

SMITH. [*Ignoring him and speaking to* MARTIN *and* RATCLIFFE.] I take my leave to go.

MARTIN. [*Looking at* WINGFIELD.] Aye.

WINGFIELD. [*Finally.*] Aye.

SMITH. We will depart within the hour. [*He turns aside and goes rapidly out at the right center.*]

WINGFIELD. Come, gentlemen, to our work at the church.

[*They move on out at the left rear. The light brightens on the* DIGGERS.]

READ. You heard what he said. Our biscuit is all spoiled!

BARRET. And ye heard Captain Smith say he would bring corn for bread from the Indians and he will.

READ. Aye, he will.

OLD EDWARD. If old Opecancanough don't ketch him.

[*They go on digging.* JONAS *moves out to the front of the scene with his mattock, the light fading from the* DIGGERS *and holding on him.*]

JONAS. And off Captain Smith went hunting for corn. Where the colony was concerned he weren't afraid of the devil hisself nor all the imps of darkness. He sailed and rowed forty miles up the river, as 'twas told, and went ashore and started marching overland. Then what some of us feared happened. Chief Opecancanough and his warriors waylaid the captain. They killed some of his men and scattered the others, and for all his fighting like a mad dog, took Captain Smith prisoner. And shouting and screeching like fiends to high heaven, they carried him along to old Powhatan's village to be killed. And our hearts bowed down in sorrow like the lonesome bulrush when we heard the news.

[*The light fades from him as he turns back into the shadows. From the darkness of the woods up at the left a wild tearing Indian yell is heard, and a drum begins to beat. The light comes up there.*]

Scene III

The forest in front of Powhatan's village near the York River. In the foreground is a tall wooden Indian god or okie some ten or twelve feet high, made from a single tree trunk, and with a nightmarish carved head set like a hideous bloom at the top of it. Farther back in the shadows the curved outline of the front of Powhatan's bark house is seen. JOHN SMITH, *surrounded by a jostling gang of Indian men and women, some of whom carry red-burning lightwood torches, is whirled out of the woods and up before the monstrous god.* OPECANCANOUGH, *a tall muscular middle-aged chief wearing a white feather cloak, is in charge. With him is his son* KOCOUM. *A frenzied clamor comes from the throats of the people, amplified in the sound track.* SMITH *is bareheaded, his clothes torn, his face and body bloodied. Two half-naked Indian men holding great clubs and wearing black masks move forward ready to beat out his brains. The medicine man* RAWHUNT *bursts in and cavorts wildly around, shaking his gourds and working up a fervor of hate and fury. The lofty figure of old* POWHATAN *comes out of his house at the rear.*

*The howling and persecution continue as the
drum throbs on.* SMITH *gazes at* POWHATAN
*in a mixture of defiant agony and pleading.
The* WOMEN *claw at him, scratch his flesh,
tear away strips of his shirt and pluck at his
beard and hair.* POWHATAN *moves on down
into the scene.* OPECANCANOUGH *steps in front
of his brother, bows in homage to him, then
with gestures fiercely demands that the prisoner be put to death,* KOCOUM *gesturing likewise. The* WOMEN *turn to* POWHATAN, *adding their pantomimic demands to* OPECANCANOUGH'S. *The old chief moves over to*
SMITH *and smiles horribly in his face and
pantomimes striking him again and again.
The people pour out their curses and imprecations, declaring in a medley of shouts and
yells that the white man is a beggarly coward,
an old squaw, that he stinks like manure and
is no more than snot from the nose.*

INDIANS. Tassentassis cuttasamais! Tumpseis! Moich pokets! Tassentassis ahtures! Makique! Makique!

[SMITH'S *shaggy head lolls from side to side, but no whimper of pain escapes him.* POWHATAN *shows his admiration. He turns to the persecutors and orders them to witness the stout heart of this man. He will die bravely even so.*]

POWHATAN. Nimetewh towah! [*The drum booms more loudly, and* POWHATAN *orders* SMITH *to be killed.*] Nepassingwahoon tsepaih!

[KOCOUM *and the* TWO WARRIORS *hasten to obey.* SMITH *is jerked to the ground as* RAWHUNT *with his gourds dances his joy. The* INDIANS *let loose a high cry, saying that the captive's bones shall be broken to pieces.*]

INDIANS. [*Led by* OPECANCANOUGH *and* KOCOUM.] Ketarowksumah! Ketarowksumah!

[SMITH'S *head is slammed down on the execution block, and the executioners step back and lift their clubs. At this moment* POCAHONTAS *rushes down the incline into the scene crying out for them to stop.*]

POCAHONTAS. Mattah! Mattah!

[*With the exception of* OPECANCANOUGH *and* KOCOUM, *the* INDIANS *react in astonishment. Some of the* MAIDS *and* WOMEN *bow their heads and step instantly back before her vehemence.* POCAHONTAS *flings herself down by* SMITH, *defying the masked men.* KOCOUM *seizes her by the arm and pulls her roughly away, gesturing for the men to proceed.* POWHATAN *reprimands* KOCOUM *for his behavior to his beloved daughter.*]

POWHATAN. Mattah, Kocoum!

[OPECANCANOUGH *appeals to those around him, but they dare not oppose* POWHATAN, *their mighty emperor.* POCAHONTAS *springs up and stands with her back to the prisoner, her arms stretched out protectingly before him.* KOCOUM *stares angrily at her. The howling dies down, but the drum continues.* OPECANCANOUGH *turns away, then charges back and beats the air with his fists in rage, howling.*]

OPECANCANOUGH. Katarowksumah! [*He points an accusing finger at* SMITH *and gestures to say that the white man has come to rob them of their land, to take away all they possess and trample them to the earth.*

THE FOUNDERS

To illustrate he throws off his white feathered cloak and stamps on it. He falls on his knees, pouring handfuls of dirt on his head in wailing lamentation. POWHATAN *hesitates.* POCAHONTAS *now falls on her knees pleading with her father that the prisoner's life be spared for her sake, marking the tears she sheds for him.*]

POCAHONTAS. [*Passionately.*] Paseme—paseme—neire miske. Nummawh! [*She points to the sky to say that the great spirit will be angry if this white man is harmed. The old chief now looks from one to the other of the kneeling figures. The* WOMEN *lean forward, and the* MEN *lower their waving angry arms and watch* POCAHONTAS *intently. The drum softens down. The torches which have been waving wildly ring the scene motionless in the air now.* POWHATAN *turns quickly over to his god to ask his will.* POCAHONTAS *crawls forward on her knees and flings her arms around her father's legs. The old man is moved at her tears. He turns back. Lifting up his great arms, he announces that she has spoken well and he agrees to her request.*]

POWHATAN. Ohcawooc! Cuppeh.

[OPECANCANOUGH *lets out a snarl of rage, turns his back on the scene and stands with his hand gripped on his tomahawk.* KOCOUM *stands by him.* POCAHONTAS *rises and runs over to* SMITH. POWHATAN *steps forward, gestures the executioners aside, and the two lift* SMITH *up.* POCAHONTAS *now takes* SMITH's *right hand and puts it against her forehead, her left hand on her heart, thus claiming him for herself. A maid hands forward a gourd of water which* POCAHONTAS *puts to* SMITH's *lips. He drinks and is refreshed. The mood of the scene has changed entirely. The lighted peace pipe is handed in.* POWHATAN *passes it to* SMITH *who takes a draw, blows smoke in the peace ritual across the chief's shoulder and hands it on to* OPECANCANOUGH.]

SMITH. Smoke the pipe of peace, Opecancanough, and let us be friends.

[OPECANCANOUGH *violently refuses it and steps into the darkness at the rear, followed by his son.* POWHATAN *takes the pipe, puffs it and blows smoke across* SMITH'S *shoulder. The drum stops beating. The* MAIDS *laugh and smile joyously.* POWHATAN *embraces* SMITH *saying they are friends now.*]

POWHATAN. Chesk chammay!

[RAWHUNT *goes over and falls down on his knees in front of his okie.* SMITH *holds himself up more strongly.*]

SMITH. Chesk chammay! Friends! We are brothers.

[POCAHONTAS *agrees eagerly that this is so.*]

POCAHONTAS. Netah! Nemat!

[SMITH *puts his right hand on his heart.* POWHATAN *and* POCAHONTAS *are jubilant, and she claps her hands happily.* SMITH *shakes his groggy head as if clearing his mind.*]

SMITH. Great Powhatan—know that my king, ruler of wide lands and seas—[*With his hands he indicates.*] —he sends many ships and men here to this his new kingdom—[*He hooks his hand in* POWHATAN's.]— with gifts for you his brothers—hoes—hatchets—even to the mighty smoking sticks—the guns—pocosacks— pocosacks. [*He simulates chopping and cutting and the firing of a gun which he hands to* POWHATAN. *The old man is happy. He slaps* SMITH *jovially on the back, half knocking him down, then lifts him quickly up as he thanks him.*]

POWHATAN. Kenah—kenah.

SMITH. My mighty werowance over the water—he says feed my people at Jamestown, give them corn. [*He simulates shelling corn, putting it into his mouth and pointing off.* POWHATAN *agrees and orders everyone to be joyful.*]

POWHATAN. Cuppeh. [*Shouting.*] Kesshekissun! Cantecante!

[A MAID *begins to play a flute, and the drum starts its light beating.* POWHATAN *leads the way up the incline, he and* POCAHONTAS *helping* SMITH *along.* POCAHONTAS *and her* MAIDS, *some of them dancing, all begin singing in high happy voices in unison, bidding their white brother, mighty man that he is, to rest now and suffer no more.*]

POCAHONTAS AND MAIDS. Oh lah ah ah—ah loh ah ah, nepaun towah nowes—werowance tassentassis nemat.

[*The procession goes on out, leaving* RAWHUNT *kneeling before the idol.* OPECANCANOUGH *re-enters swiftly and raises his tomahawk in the air. Some of the* WARRIORS *who have started away with* POWHATAN *turn back and run to him. He brings his tomahawk down simulating braining an enemy. Beckoning to the* WARRIORS, *he dashes away into the forest. They follow him. The light begins to fade. In the distance the jubilant clamor of the Indians is heard as they feast* SMITH *and celebrate his adoption into their tribe. The scene fades out. There is a moment of darkness, and the light comes up on the woodland stage at the right.*]

Scene IV

JONAS PROFIT *is standing with his spade in a patch of potato ground at the edge of the forest. His musket is nearby. His clothes are patched and tattered now from the wear and tear of time. He looks out at the audience.*

JONAS. [*Ironically.*] Brave and promising words Captain Smith spoke—that day when the Indians were about to beat out his brains and Pocahontas saved his life and 'dopted him into the tribe. [*In somewhat satirical imitation.*] Yea, the mighty king over the waters will send many ships and men to his new kingdom Virginia and with gifts of axes and hoes and guns for our brothers, the Indians. [*Imitating* POWHATAN.] Oom—oom, and I, the great Powhatan, will feed your people at Jamestown from the stores of my corn, and all will be like sweet doves cooing in the dell. [*Shaking his head and indicating himself.*] Well, you can see from the looks of me, Jonas Profit, it didn't turn out that way—me with my old clothes patched together this winter and summer that's past, and digging this potato patch here that's been dug over twenty times before. [*Taking a step forward and holding his spade.*] Old Powhatan sent corn for a while, but when he didn't get the guns, the smoking sticks, he was promised, he stopped. Then Captain Smith was blowed up by gunpowder soon after and sent home by the wrangling

THE FOUNDERS 41

council to answer charges for getting his men killed.

Ships have come and gone and brought more colonists here, a few women—with Mistress Temperance Flowerdew amongst 'em—and a handful of pitiful children too, and some supplies which never lasted long with all the starving, dying mouths.

President has succeeded president—after Wingfield, Ratcliffe—then Matthew Scrivener, and next Captain Smith hisself—all gone from here, beaten by the wilderness, and poor Captain George Percy, now named governor instead of president, he holds us together as best he can. Afflictions have poured down upon us—hunger and cold and death. Thus we have lived for months and months with no word from England. Sir Thomas Gates with his ship has never come—him and Captain Yeardley and Master Rolfe and their supply that was set to sail here. But Mistress Temperance Flowerdew— [*Nodding his head toward the center stage.*]—Captain Yeardley's love that was to wed him on his coming—keeps up her hope. Brave she is and through all this starving time has helped tend the sick and dying. And Pocahontas, that strange heathen maid, has brung what food she could slip away from her suspicious old father. Even now she's in the fort there with a little sodden corn—and some of her herbs and salves for the feeble ones.

[SERGEANT JEFFREY ABBOT, LAYDON, DODS *and a few other men come down the incline in a line carrying a long fish net.* WILLIAM WHITE *and* WILLIAM GARRET *are behind armed with muskets.* JONAS *looks out.*]

JONAS. What news, Sergeant Abbot?

[ABBOT *is a young man of 25 with a lean hawk-like face and ice-cold eyes.*]

ABBOT. With the twilight falling we thought best to come in. We spied an Indian canoe skulking on the river.

JONAS. They spy after Pocahontas as well as us.

DODS. We hung a monstrous sturgeon, but he broke our net in our weakness and went flopping away.

[*The chapel bell begins to toll from the darkness of the center stage. The* MEN *stop an instant, some of them taking off their ragged hats in respect.*]

LAYDON. Who goes to the grave now?

DODS. It matters not, 'twill be one of us next.

[ABBOT *leads the way on, and they all go down into the darkness.* JONAS *looks out before him again.*]

JONAS. Our men must fish and grabble for roots as best they can with the soldiers warding. Old Powhatan stays hid growling away in the forest, plotting none knows what, and Opecancanough's men ring us round waiting for us to die, finding it cheaper than spilling his warriors' blood before the few guns we still have. And die we do. Aye, the hardest heart bleeds to hear the pitiful murmurings and outcries of our people as they depart this life, their bodies trailed out of their cabins in the morning like dogs to be buried. Captain Gosnold of the council is dead and gone, and mad Captain Kendall shot for treason against us. On the sixth John Asbie died of the bloody flix, and then George Flowre of the swelling, and next William Brewster, gentleman, of a wound by the savages. And Jerome Alicock, and Francis Midwinter, Edward Morish, Edward Browne dead too, and Stephen Galthorpe of a poisonous

THE FOUNDERS

sarpint, and Rosa Lambert and Mary Bradley of the fever, and Edward Harrington and George Walker and Captain Martin's young and only son, and Thomas Studley, our cape merchant, and our beloved minister Master Hunt—and others to a frightful number. Of the three hundred that have come here only sixty of us wretched ones remain alive. [*Stoutly.*] But yet we man this fort. And as Governor Percy says, long as we keep Jamestown, then England holds Virginia. Aye, brave hearts are still here, though help must soon come or all is ended like the Lost Colony at Roanoke. [*Mockingly.*] There comes a valiant brave heart now—our ancient friend Sir Austin Cooms.

[*The voice of* AUSTIN COOMS *is heard in the forest at the rear raised in a stave of croaking song.*]

AUSTIN.

> When Sampson was a tall young man
> His power and strength increased then,
> And in the host and tribe of Dan,
>   The Lord did bless him alway.

[AUSTIN *comes down the incline and behind him a disgusted sweaty* PHARAOH *stripped to the waist and carrying a bag of dirt over his shoulder. The fop is much changed but still carries himself somewhat pridefully. His once fine clothes are so no longer, and the pink parasol he holds over his head to shade him from the heat is a wreck with the ribs showing through. In one hand he clutches a large bouquet of native wild flowers—black-eyed Susans, Queen Anne's lace, yarrow and eglantine.*]

PHARAOH. [*Somewhat defiantly.*] Nay, no further, I tell ye, Master Austin.

AUSTIN. [*Encouraging him along.*] Patience, dear Pharaoh, faithful Pharaoh. We'll soon be to the fort.

JONAS. [*Indulgently.*] Digging for gold again, Sir Austin?

AUSTIN. For certain I've found it this time or Governor Percy may set me in the stocks for a heathen Turk.

[PHARAOH *stumbles and drops the bag angrily down.*]

We were digging roots with the others there when I saw the sly glittering in the dirt.

PHARAOH. All ablaze and in a fury master was, and nothing for it but we must load up and fetch it along quick to William Dawson, the refiner.

AUSTIN. And this time he will tell ye true we've discovered a rich mine.

JONAS. There's no gold in this ground, Master Austin. The glitter is naught but little crystals in the sand when the sun strikes it. Master Dawson and Abram Ransacke too have told thee so.

PHARAOH. Ah-hah! And I be done with it!

AUSTIN. [*Fanning his face with the bouquet of flowers.*] Too many cowards and weak of will are in this settlement, Jonas Profit. They yield over the struggle too soon. But Austin Cooms—I do not yield. Let them laugh at me, let my servant grow rebellious—

PHARAOH. Me?

AUSTIN. Aye, to thy undoing. Hear me—if we discover gold this colony is saved. We have found no passage for trade to the South Seas nor converted any Indians. Not one penny of profit has the Virginia Company ever had back in England. Find but a touch of gold and our troubles are over! The sea will be crowded with ships flying to the New World and the settlement be strong forevermore. So I keep searching, searching. Seventy times seven, it sayeth in the Bible. Sometimes, Jonas Profit, it seemeth I be the only true friend of this colony. I never cease laboring for its salvation.

[*A number of* COLONISTS *come down the incline in front of them and pass on by carrying empty baskets and a bucket or two. Some of them are gnawing roots they have dug up.* READ *and* WEBB *follow along wardingly behind them with their muskets. One of the colonists,* BARRET, *totters from weakness.* PHARAOH *suddenly steps over and helps him along.* AUSTIN *calls out.*]

AUSTIN. Come back here, Pharaoh!

PHARAOH. Nay, I will carry that fool's earth no longer.

AUSTIN. Fool's earth! [*Furiously.*] I command ye! [*He runs after* PHARAOH, *but* READ *puts his gun in front of him and stops him. The procession goes on into the darkness.* AUSTIN *turns forlornly back to* JONAS.] Merciful Lord in heaven, what are things coming to in this wild land—when a bond servant turns against his own master! [*He steps over and looks down at the bag.*] Bear it on for me, Jonas, and ye shall have a share of it.

JONAS. Nay, Sir Austin, I dig over this ground again hoping for a potato for little Martha Raynor that lies stretched and moaning in her bed.

[AUSTIN *strains at the bag, lays down his flowers and strains again.* JONAS *helps him get the load up onto his shoulder.*]

AUSTIN. [*In doleful disgust.*] Let it be Sir Austin no more, Jonas Profit, for I am sore beat and battered about and in the shame of this my menial labor all my titles and honor be taken away.

JONAS. Then ye will walk the more lightly for it.

[AUSTIN *starts on off, and* JONAS *picks up the flowers.*]

Your flowers. [*He hands them to* AUSTIN.]

AUSTIN. I gathered these for the little Nat Peacock, the last boy left to us. I promised them for his sick eyes.

JONAS. I fear he will not see them where's he's gone. I heard the bell tolling even now for his burying.

AUSTIN. Day by day they die.

JONAS. Aye—yesterday Henry Morton, Thomas Hope and Ezra Parker. And the day before that Dius O'Connor, Alec Short and James Blewett. Poor Barbara Blewett—her heart is broke for her man.

AUSTIN. [*Sorrowfully as he smells the flowers.*] A sweet lad, Nat was, and carried the crozier faithful for Master Hunt that's passed the pearly gates. On Sunday mornings in the chapel he would sing out loud and clear, "Holy angels now descending." I will put them on his grave. [*He goes off spraddle-legged down the incline into the darkness.*]

JONAS. [*To the air.*] Yea, and let them put a guard around that grave. Monstrous horror though it be—bodies have been dug up of late by hungry midnight ghouls—so doth misery turn a man into a beast. Ah Lord! [*He shudders and spits, then returns to his digging, the light fading down on him. From the center stage the voice of* GOVERNOR PERCY *is heard reading the funeral service, and a gray foggy twilight comes up there. We see a group of forlorn* COLONISTS *gathered in front of the little chapel which projects slightly in now at the left rear on the upper level. In front of the church a number of pitiful crosses are stuck up. We do not see much of the setting other than the space around the front of the church. We faintly glimpse a stretch of palisades in the background with the leaning figure of* BRINTON *aloft on the walkway standing guard there. The people are facing* PERCY *with their backs to the audience, thus shutting out the actual business of the burial.* PERCY *is reading from the prayer-book, his tall thin humped-over shoulders covered by an old ragged cloak.*]

PERCY. Blessed are the dead which die in the Lord, even so saith the spirit, they rest from their labors.

PEOPLE. [*In a husky wooden response.*] Even so saith the Lord.

PERCY. We give thanks to thee, O Lord, that thou hast delivered from the miseries of this wretched world and from the body of death and all temptation this thy servant.

PEOPLE. [*As before.*] Blessed be our God.

PERCY. When the breath of man goeth forth he shall turn again to his earth and all his thoughts perish. [*Stretching out his hands.*] Into this ground, consecrated by the bones of our piteous dead, we place the body of this little boy—to await the resurrection of his spotless soul in Heaven.

[AUSTIN *comes in at the right with his flowers and joins the group. A few of the* COLONISTS *bend over as if lowering a coffin into the grave.* AUSTIN *pushes up among them as* PERCY *continues and the scene begins to fade.*]

For the trumpet shall blow and the dead shall rise incorruptible and death shall be swallowed up in victory. I believe to see the goodness of the Lord—

PEOPLE. [*Still as before.*] In the land of the living. [*The people begin singing a hymn of lamentation in a pleading, halting harmony.*]

> O Lord, in thee is all my trust,
>   Give ear unto my woeful cry.
> Refuse me not that am unjust
>   But bowing down thy heav'nly eye,
> Behold how I do still lament—

[*The scene fades on down and out, the singing dies away, and the light comes up on* JONAS *again at his digging.*]

JONAS. [*Strongly.*] And Governor Percy there says brave words too—death shall be swallowed up in victory. Aye, mayhap in the world beyond the skies. What we need is a victory over death here at Jamestown. [*Low under the earth far away a rumble of thunder sounds.*] There it goes again—another one of them thunderstorms a-brewing. Merciful goodness! And our roofs rotting down with holes in 'em you could throw a cat through—if we had a cat. But bless my soul, John Dods and Tom Barret et him. The Lord has persecuted us enough without sending hail and sleet and snow to fall on us in winter and thunderbolts and balls of fire in summer from above. [*He turns and kicks the ground disgustedly.*] There's never a 'tater here any more than the pearl of great price itself. [*With a shout he grabs up a little potato which his foot has uncovered.*] Blessed be God, I've found one! [*He holds the potato and kisses it. The thunder rumbles angrily again in the distance. He looks up at the sky and salutes.*] Aye, Old Master, I hear your voice. Of late I had begun to doubt thee like so many others here. But now with this little token of thy mercy I take heart again. Thou art still with us—I trust.

[*With his spade he goes down the incline toward the center stage. A flash of lightning breaks in the sky and the thunder booms nearer. The light comes slowly up at the right front as* JONAS *enters and we see him cross the scene over to the left and out. Twenty or thirty* COLONISTS *are now revealed gathered at the right, some sitting on old casks or boxes, some lying on the ground, others sitting bowed over on the upper level at the rear and still others stirring restlessly and weakly about here and there. A dull fire is burning around a big iron pot in which the fresh bit of corn* POCAHONTAS *has brought has been boiled.* TEMPERANCE FLOWERDEW, *23, and* BARBARA BLEWETT, *25, are going about with pewter cups and gourds, feeding the weaker colonists.* TEMPERANCE *is an attractive young woman with dark hair and hollow dark eyes. She has suffered through many a weary month, nursing the sick and the dying, enduring hunger and cold like the others. And though her face and figure are frightfully worn, she still keeps up her spirit and determination.* BARBARA *is a young widow in black, with a rather large, round and sweetly piteous countenance.* COLONISTS *are coming haltingly up now and then, dipping their cups and gourds into the pot and moving away.* TEMPERANCE *takes a cup to* ANNE LAYDON, *16, who sits close by holding her baby to her.*]

ANNE. [*Taking it.*] Thankee, Mistress Flowerdew. [*Lifting up her baby and putting the cup to her lips.*] Drink, little Virginia. Drink, my darling.

[BARBARA *takes the cup to ailing* JOHN MARTIN *who stands leaning on his stick over at the left center, an old piece of sailcloth over his shoulders.*]

BARBARA. Master Martin.

[MARTIN *nods his thanks and takes the cup. The light brightens a bit on the cabin at the left front, and we see into the little building as if the wall were off. A few rough bunks are within, a number of sick people occupying them, and one or two sitting on the floor. On the near bed lies* THOMAS FOREST, *a man of middle age. His wife,* LUCY, *a few years younger, is standing by him, fanning him with her tattered apron.* POCAHONTAS, *with one of her maids, is poulticing his chest. Another* INDIAN MAID *stands by with a willow basket of herbs.*]

LUCY. Take heart, dear husband. Pocahontas will make you well with her medicines.

FOREST. [*To* POCAHONTAS, *quaveringly.*] Bless you, bless you, my child.

[POCAHONTAS *and her* MAIDS *turn back to the rear of the room with their basket and begin doctoring other* COLONISTS. TEMPERANCE *enters with a cup.* LUCY *takes it and lifting her husband's head, puts it to his lips. Hands are reached from the rough beds at* TEMPERANCE.]

VOICES. Me! Me!—Please! Please!

TEMPERANCE. Anon, anon.

[BARBARA *comes in with a large gourd and goes from one to the other of the sick ones feeding them. The storm continues to rise, with thunder and lightning and the whooming wind.* TEMPERANCE *returns to the pot. The light comes up somewhat in the little court of guard building at the right where* SERGEANT ABBOT *and a few of his* SOLDIERS *are standing or sitting about with their muskets, and drinking from their cups and gourds.*]

DODS. [*Retching.*] Nay, I've swallowed wind so long my belly won't take this watery stuff. [*He sets the tin aside, and* GARRET *picks it up.*]

GARRET. 'Tis better than that salt-sea river water.

[*He drains the cup, tastes it, and then with his hand to his mouth, rises and stumbles out at the rear to get rid of it. Another flash of lightning tears across the sky out on the river, followed by a crash of thunder.* ANNE *lets out a little scream, stands up and sits moaning down again. A number of people murmur and mutter and turn toward the rear looking apprehensively off. A blast of wind suddenly tears through the fort, rattling the thatch and wildly waving the tattered pieces of sailcloth with which some of the broken walls of the cabin and court of guard building are curtained.* AUSTIN COOMS *comes up to the pot and gets a serving.* JONAS *re-enters now at the left, comes over to the pot and squats down by the fire carefully placing his potato in the ashes. One or two men move up to look. He gestures them away. The wind roars in through the fort again and passes on. Suddenly the two men jerk* JONAS *away from the fire. One of them,* WHITE, *snatches the potato out of the ashes and the other leaps on him. They fight over it.* JONAS *tries to pull them apart.*]

JONAS. Give that potato back! It's for the sick girl!

[*At the word "potato" others run over. Almost instantly a number of men are rolling and clutching and clawing and choking one another on the ground, growling like dogs and banging away with their fists.* SERGEANT ABBOT *runs out of the guard house with two or three* SOLDIERS. *They dash among the men, pulling them apart, some of them raising the butts of their muskets as if to strike them.*]

ABBOT. [*Yelling above the storm.*] Cease, ye villains, I command ye! [*Some of the men are now jerked to their feet.*]

MARTIN. Peace, peace! [*He moves shakily among the irate men.*]

TEMPERANCE. Shame, shame on you all!

JONAS. [*Pointing at* WHITE.] He has eaten it. [*He tries to fly at* WHITE, *but two* SOLDIERS *hold him back.* ABBOT *grabs the guilty man by the collar.*]

ABBOT. Set him in the stocks and mayhap the lightning will strike him for a just punishment.

WHITE. [*Screaming.*] I am starving—starving!

ABBOT. So are we all. Take him away.

[WHITE *is dragged and pushed toward the rear and fastened in the stocks there.* POCAHONTAS *and her* MAIDS *come out of the cabin. They stand looking laughingly on at the turmoiling people. The storm now hits the fort in all its fury of wind and lightning and bellowing thunder. Some of the* WOMEN *scream, and moans break out more loudly from the lips of a number of* COLONISTS. *They begin clustering together in a group at the rear as if for mutual protection.*]

THE FOUNDERS

VOICES. God save us! Save us!

OTHER VOICES. Mercy, mercy! Lord have mercy upon us!

[*Two or three of the sick ones in the cabin at the left weakly climb from their bunks and stand clinging to the walls looking out, shaking with fear.* PERCY *appears at the left leaning on his stick, accompanied by* CAPTAIN POWELL.]

POWELL. [*Yelling at* ABBOT.] See to the pinnace, Sergeant Abbot. Make all fast! The governor commands it.

ABBOT. [*Shouting.*] Come on, men! [*He and a few men hurry out at the right behind the court of guard building.*]

PERCY. [*Calling out in his quavering voice.*] To your shelters, everyone!

MARTIN. Seek shelter! Seek shelter!

PERCY. [*His voice almost swallowed in the wind and the torrents of rain that have begun to fall.*] Into the house of God! It's safer there!

[TEMPERANCE, BARBARA *and others start helping the weaker ones along. In the flashes of lightning,* BRINTON *can be seen on the rampart at the rear bowed over before the gale and holding onto one of the palisades, the rain streaming from him. The culprit* WHITE *is likewise discerned sitting slumped in the stocks at the right rear. A few of the people begin running right and left like leaves blown before a storm. But most of them continue to make their way up toward the church. A few still sit by the sputtering frying fire in an apathy of hopelessness and suction of death. Two* SOLDIERS *drag in a piece of sailcloth and cover the pot and fire. The tempest of rain and wind and lightning continues with the frightful cannonading of thunder.* LAYDON *is seen putting his arm around* ANNE *and helping her with her baby up the incline. A section of the roof of the cabin at the left collapses and crashes to the ground. The sick ones left there cringe away from the deluge that pours in on them.*]

POWELL. Into the church, everybody. Away, away!

VOICES. To the church!

[*The wet and bedraggled people are now going up into the church.* JONAS *and* AUSTIN *assist the invalids out of the cabin and off toward the church.* LUCY *and* PHARAOH *half-lift and half-carry* FOREST *up to safety. The storm is now at its height.* ABBOT *and his men come pushing in at the right rear, leaning into the gale as they move, the water streaming from their caps and coats.*]

ABBOT. [*Shouting.*] The pinnace has been dashed ashore and broken!

[*He runs over to the pot where a single colonist is sitting and starts to pull him away to the rear. The colonist topples over to the ground and lies still. He is dead.* ABBOT *stands gazing down at him an instant, then he and* DODS *lift the body and bear it off to the church.* POCAHONTAS *and her* MAIDS *begin waving their hands in the air and looking up at the sky.* POCAHONTAS *takes a tobacco leaf from the basket, pinches off pieces from it and casts them into the air. Then the three of them start beating their palms together and hopping around in a circle in a weird rain dance, calling out thanks to the great God in the sky for sending this good rain which will provide fine crops and much food for his people to eat—corn and tobacco and chinquapins.*]

POCAHONTAS AND MAIDS. [*Their shrill chanting mixing in with the storm.*] Montoac peatchah—wingan camzowan—moowchick maize, tuckahoe, chinquapins mecher!

[*The remaining people outside the church on the upper level turn and look at them fearfully.*]

ABBOT. [*Jeering.*] Fear not, peoples, Pocahontas there is quieting the storm with her magic!

[PERCY *turns back and calls out sternly.*]

PERCY. Stop these blasphemous rites! Come pray with us here in the house of God, I beg you, Pocahontas!

POCAHONTAS. [*Almost fiercely as she points up.*] Our God—great spirit—the one God. He sends rain for much corn.

PERCY. [*Loudly.*] You will be destroyed by his wrath.

[*He shakes his stick in the air.* POCAHONTAS *looks at him, and then she and her* MAIDS *break into sudden and merry laughter and go turning rapidly out at the left, carrying on their shrill chanting.* PERCY *turns and enters the church. A hymn of piety and faith has been started there, led by* TEMPERANCE, JONAS *and* BARBARA, *and inside at the front, lighted by lightning flashes, we see many of the people kneeling, stretching out their hands and beating their breasts, their faces upraised in pleading to God.* PERCY *is holding his Bible aloft as if to console them.*]

TEMPERANCE AND OTHERS. [*Singing.*]
> The Lord is my only support
> And he that doth me feed,
> How then can I lack anything
> Whereof I stand in need!

[*Other voices come in, among them* AUSTIN'S *shrill tenor, and as the singing gathers volume it begins, as it were, to wage a struggle with the elements outside.*]

PEOPLE.
> And when I feel myself near lost
> Then doth he home me take,
> Conducting me in his right paths
> E'en for his own name's sake.

[*As the people sing, they gradually begin standing up straight, their faces raised in growing confidence and certitude in the Almighty's protection.*]

> And though I were e'en at death's door
> Yet would I feel no ill,
> For by thy rod and shepherd's crook
> I am comforted still.

[*The storm begins to decrease in violence, the lightning flashes occurring less often and the thunder reverberating farther and farther away.*]

> And finally while breath doth last
> Thy grace shall me defend,
> And in the house of God will I
> My life forever spend. Amen!

[*The storm is fading out now, the last of the cloud passing over, and from the west the rays of the setting sun bathe the top of the palisades and the cross-surmounted church in a warm suffusion of rosy light. Off at the right a halloo sounds, and then is repeated.* BRINTON *on the walkway straightens up and looks off.*]

BRINTON. Who goes there!

A VOICE. [*In the distance.*] Open up! Halloo! Halloo! Open the gates! [*The people come hurrying out of the church.*]

MARTIN. An English voice!

[*A heavy knocking is heard against the palisades gate off-scene.* PERCY *gestures, and* POWELL *and* ABBOT *run off at the right.*]

VOICES. [*In a gabble.*] They come. [*Wildly.*] The ship has come! They've come!

OTHER VOICES. Our countrymen have come!

[*The people keep pushing out of the church, crowding toward the right, hugging one another excitedly.* PERCY *comes down the incline, and* MARTIN *and others of the council move to his side. The people who a moment before were hysterical and groveling with fear, are shouting and cheering now, their cries breaking in the air.*]

VOICES. We are saved! Saved! [*Some of them beat their hands together and weep with happiness.*] We will have food.

OTHER VOICES. Food! Food!

[CAPTAIN GEORGE YEARDLEY, JOHN ROLFE *and six or eight men burst in at the right.* POWELL *and* ABBOT *hurry along behind them.* YEARDLEY *is a lithe-figured man of 31, with a frank, engaging and somewhat impetuous manner.* ROLFE *is about 26, a little above medium height and by contrast more serious and de-*

liberate. YEARDLEY *stops before* PERCY *and his group.*]

YEARDLEY. I am Captain George Yeardley. Sir Thomas Gates sends his greetings, sir, from his ship anchored down the river. With Master John Rolfe here and these brave men we have come ahead in the long boat. [PERCY *reaches out his hand and* YEARDLEY *grasps it.*]

PERCY. God's blessing on thee, Captain Yeardley, for your deliverance—and for ours.

MARTIN. We had given Sir Thomas and all up for dead.

YEARDLEY. We were cast away on the Bermoothes—ten months agone—our ship stuck fast on a rock. We built two other small ones that brought us here. Aye, Master Rolfe.

ROLFE. They have rode out the storm down the river there and will sail in tomorrow as the dawn gives light.

[*A murmur of disappointment rises among the people.*]

VOICES. Tomorrow! Tomorrow!

PERCY. [*Sternly.*] Then we can endure one night more.

[YEARDLEY'S *eyes are searching the scene. He spies* TEMPERANCE, *and pushing through the clamoring people runs over to her. She rushes into his arms with a broken cry.*]

TEMPERANCE. Thank God, thank God! Oh—all the days and all the nights I prayed for your safety. [*She clings to him weeping.*]

YEARDLEY. And me for you. Ever on the cruel waters my thoughts were with you here. [*He kisses her. The people crowd around the newcomers, shaking their hands, embracing them, gazing at them as if they were miraculous beings.* YEARDLEY, *his arm around* TEMPERANCE, *turns to* PERCY.] And these valiant men who have fought the raging river and heaven's water spouts to bring our long boat through—I commend them to your favor, Governor Percy.

PERCY. All honor to you men—each and all.

[*The men nod wearily, staring at him.*]

PEOPLE. Cheers for the brave men! Cheers! [*A few hats and caps are thrown up if feebly.* YEARDLEY *and* TEMPERANCE *move toward the rear.*]

ROLFE. [*To* PERCY.] And as they pulled at the oars, they shouted cheerily above the roaring storm—stroke, stroke—for food awaits us at Jamestown. They are faint with their great labor, sir, and hungry. If you would but kindly feed them.

[*A pall falls on the people.* PERCY *stares at him.*]

PERCY. Feed them?

ROLFE. They are most worthy of your care.

[PERCY *looks blankly about him.*]

VOICES. Hungry! He says they are hungry!

ROLFE. Our long stay on the islands, sir, brought our stores nigh to naught. We have been on short rations these two weeks to reach here.

[*The people look at one another in horror.* BARBARA BLEWETT *begins to laugh hysterically.* JONAS *turns and tenderly quiets her.*]

MARTIN. Look about you, John Rolfe. We have no food.

[ROLFE *gazes out at them and then at his men.*]

ROLFE'S MEN. [*With a groan.*] They have no food.

[*The people now crowd toward* ROLFE.]

PEOPLE. Feed us! Feed us!

[ROLFE'S *men suddenly shout back at them.*]

MEN. Feed us! Feed us!

PERCY AND ROLFE. Silence, people, silence.

ROLFE. Patience, men.

ANNE. [*Shrieking.*] My baby will die here! [LAYDON *puts his arm around her and they go out at the left. Some of the others begin to wander disconsolately off.*]

ROLFE. Take heart, ye all. What food we have on the ship, I know his excellency will share with you.

[PERCY *gestures to* ABBOT *with his stick.*]

PERCY. Give the men of this.

[*The sailcloth is lifted off the pot, and the men crowd eagerly forward.* ABBOT *and* ROLFE *begin helping them. They do their best at drinking. Some of them turn away.*]

ROLFE. Let us be thankful that we have found our countrymen alive! [*Looking about at the tattered forlorn figures.*] They have suffered more than we.

FIRST MAN. That could not be, Master Rolfe. [*He stands holding his cup in his hand, staring at it.*]

THE FOUNDERS

PERCY. To your cabins, good people. Tomorrow we will take counsel for your safety and welfare with our new governor, Sir Thomas Gates, when he lands. Be of good cheer. Our long nightmare is ended. Sergeant Abbot, release the prisoner.

[*The people move off at the right and left and some to the rear by the church.* ABBOT *lets* WHITE *out of the stocks and sends him up to relieve* BRINTON *on the walkway.* YEARDLEY *and* TEMPERANCE *come toward the front.*]

Captain Yeardley, I offer you the comfort of my poor cabin.

YEARDLEY. My thanks, sir. [*To* ROLFE.] See to our men, Master Rolfe. [PERCY, MARTIN, POWELL *and others go away at the left.* ROLFE *lays aside his soaking coat and beats his wet hat against his knee.* YEARDLEY *and* TEMPERANCE *linger at the left front.*] To look into your eyes again, to hear your voice, to kiss you—an ever-haunting dream. And now I hold your hand, it seems I never had that dream.

TEMPERANCE. I dreamed you came to me undrownded by the sea—every night I dreamed that dream. And now you're here 'tis even more a dream. [*They move on out at the left.*]

ABBOT. [*To* ROLFE.] I will give you and your men what poor shelter I can, Master Rolfe. [*Gesturing.*] You see to what desolation this colony has come.

ROLFE. [*Fervently.*] I do. And the heart in me stops, melted at the sight of this misery. Then it beats strong again in pride to think that ye have held firm in this glorious enterprise.

ABBOT. [*Satirically.*] Hundreds have come here in this glorious enterprise, and the earth has devoured all but this handful.

ROLFE. [*Strongly, evangelically.*] The new nation a-building here will someday honor you, and the story of your heroism shall brighten a page of history forevermore.

ABBOT. Hah! [*Abruptly.*] You men come with me.

[*The men rise and follow him wearily off at the right rear.* JONAS *punches up the fire. Now that we see* ROLFE *better, he shows to be a young man with good strong shoulders—if he had any flesh on them—long arms, big bony workman's hands and a grave, preoccupied face. His reddish hair is unkempt and tangled, and his eyes below heavy sun-bleached brows are a misty blue. There is about him an air of self-absorption, of one who carries on in the depths of himself an intense and personal inner life. And he does—as we shall find out—an inner life of devout concentration on the work he wants to do and faith in his God who confirms him in that intent. Now and then, however, when something especially pleases him, his gravity will relax and his countenance beam with sunny joyousness, but only for a little while, when his pious gravity will take control again.*]

ROLFE. [*The words breaking from him.*] Jamestown—Virginia, Virginia—Jamestown, magic words! This the brave new world. And it is that—land of my long hoping and desiring—of poems writ and ballads sung. And after weary wandering like Ulysses of old, my feet are planted on thy shore. And by the sacrifice of those before me, in the name of my poor loved ones buried afar,

I swear my consecration even unto death to the task ahead. [*He looks piously up.*]

JONAS. Amen. [ROLFE *turns and looks at him.*] It is well for this settlement thou art come, Master John Rolfe—thee and thy faith.

ROLFE. I come to labor as I can. [*He fishes a pipe out of his pocket and lights it from the ember* JONAS *holds.* POCAHONTAS *and her two* MAIDS *enter at the left. One of them carries a lighted torch and the willow basket and the other an empty corn hamper.* ROLFE *stares at* POCAHONTAS *as if he had seen an apparition. He points at her with his pipe.*] It cannot be—nay—you are—Pocahontas! [POCAHONTAS *nods. He goes on jubilantly.*] In my mind I was wont to see thee—coming through the forest with thy maids—bringing food to Jamestown—and laughing and singing. It's in Captain Smith's book I read in England till I know it by rote. Now I meet thee, angel of mercy.

[*He puffs his pipe excitedly.* JONAS *steps up close to him and inhales some of the smoke.* POCAHONTAS *laughs.* ROLFE *sees* JONAS *inhaling and hands him the pipe.* JONAS *takes several deep draws, holding the smoke in him, and then returns the pipe to* ROLFE *who is still gazing at* POCAHONTAS.]

POCAHONTAS. You bring strong men—many—and save the people.

ROLFE. She speaks English!

JONAS. Captain Smith taught her words when he was here—and Thomas Savage and Mistress Flowerdew since.

ROLFE. [*Eagerly.*] I know words of your language,

Pocahontas—from Captain Smith's book—Paseme uppowoc—Give me some tobacco. [*He holds the pipe toward her, but she shakes her head.*]

POCAHONTAS. [*With a gay little childish laugh.*] Kenah —thank you.

JONAS. She is wondrous quick in her wits, Master Rolfe.

POCAHONTAS. [*Pointing to* ROLFE'S *pipe and saying the tobacco he smokes is good.*] Wingutsee uppowoc. I like.

ROLFE. Aye, good Spanish tobacco. I have brought seed from the Bermoothes to plant here. If it thrive and have proper curing, then England may buy from us, not Spain, and there be much trade.

JONAS. [*Now letting out the great cloud of smoke he has held within him.*] She brings us the Indian weed. She knows the curing of it.

ROLFE. Then mayhap she can teach me the method. [*Turning to her.*] Teach me—teach—

[*She nods and suddenly takes his hand and puts it on her head.*]

POCAHONTAS. [*Smiling up in his face.*] Master Rolfe I like.

[ROLFE *pulls his hand away in embarrassment. She laughs again, and the* MAIDS *giggle. The three suddenly dart up the incline and into the woods.*]

ROLFE. Where doth she fare in the drear night?

JONAS. Through the forest home.

ROLFE. [*Alarmed.*] Without protection?

JONAS. The night is her friend. No one would dare harm her.

[ROLFE *takes a few steps after her and stops. He lifts his hand, then turns back to* JONAS.]

ROLFE. Has her soul yet been baptized in the church?

JONAS. I say not. She won't put foot in that there chapel—scared of our God that makes bad magic there, she says. Governor Percy can't persuade her.

ROLFE. [*Sternly.*] A heathen.

JONAS. Would we Christians were half as good.

ROLFE. Then I will persuade her. Yea, I will instruct her in God's holy word.

JONAS. [*Chuckling.*] And she will teach thee to cure tobacco. A just exchange.

[*He goes on out at the right rear.* ROLFE *looks after him, then suddenly kneels down in devout prayer.*]

ROLFE. [*In sweet and personal communication with his Maker.*] Blessed be thou, my heavenly Father, for now the cup of my joy runneth over. At last I am vouchsafed to begin my labors in this thy new vineyard. [*He continues praying silently and fervently.* OLD EDWARD, *the night watchman, comes in at the rear with his pike and lighted lantern.*]

OLD EDWARD. [*In a high melodious call.*] All is well! All is well! The night is fair—the air is sweet—and all is quiet in the city! [*He stops and looks over at* ROLFE'S *kneeling figure.*]

ROLFE. [*Finishing his prayer.*] I ask it in the name of our blessed Redeemer, thy Son Jesus Christ. [*He rises and goes quietly out at the right rear.* OLD EDWARD *resumes his call.*]

OLD EDWARD. God save his majesty the king—and all is quiet in Jamestown.

[*He moves on away at the left rear behind the church, repeating his call as he goes. The light holds in a gray foggy glow on the scene. The organ begins a weird rendering of* AUSTIN COOMS' *song—croompy and staccato. A faint white nebulous light rises around the little burying plot at the rear. Creeping in as if in rhythm to the organ come two crouching figures carrying shovels. They look this way and that, then slip up to the new-made grave. They lift their shovels and start to dig. The organ continues. A touch of light shows* WHITE *above on the rampart lifting his head, listening and looking about in the night. He suddenly calls out.*]

WHITE. Ho! Stand there! [*He spies the ghouls at their work. Jerking up his musket, he fires at them. They skeet away into the shadows, the organ sounding a whorl of cascading treble notes to follow their flight.* ABBOT *and two* SOLDIERS *dash in.* WHITE *calls down to him.*] They were even at the boy's grave, Sergeant Abbot.

[ABBOT *runs to the right, looks off and then comes back.*]

ABBOT. We are no longer human here. [*To the* SOLDIERS.] Stand guard here through the night.

[*From different parts of the darkness of the fort voices*

of the COLONISTS *disturbed by the firing of the gun are heard.*]

VOICES. What is it? What's happened? Is it the Indians!

ABBOT. [*Calling loudly through the scene.*] Back to your sleep, ye people! 'Tis naught! Rest, rest!

[*The voices die away.* ABBOT *throws up his hand in a gesture of desperation and goes abruptly back the way he came. The two* SOLDIERS *take up their weary watch by the grave. Up on the rampart* WHITE *begins reloading his musket as the scene fades out. The organ reprises a few bars of the colonist hymn, "The Lord Is My Only Support," and dies. The light rises on the left incline as* JONAS *and* LAYDON *enter there from the woods. They are armed with muskets. They have been hunting but have returned empty-handed.* LAYDON *goes on down into the darkness, toward the fort.* JONAS *stops.*]

JONAS. No longer human here. Aye. [*Looking out at the audience.*] Still for all our sufferings and sins, soon after the governor landed we had a wedding—a quiet one, ye might know—between Mistress Flowerdew and Captain Yeardley, bless their two faithful hearts that had waited so long. Well, the new governor Gates strengthened us somewhat by the bit of food he issued unto us, and he sent the more able-bodied of us with all speed to fish in the river and to hunt in the forest for venison and wild turkeys, hoping to add to our store and hoping mostly in vain. The rest that were strong enough were put to repairing and caulking his ship which had took a fearful beating from the storm. And Master Rolfe, with all his praying and psalm-singing, went swift to work planting his precious tobacco seed and digging up a plot of ground to set his crop later. Pocahontas come back to visit the sick, and she helped him at his labor. And he besought her much about Christ and him crucified—[*Chuckling.*]—and about other things. I heard him at it. From the first he was all eyes for her and she for him. Mystery, mystery. And from the first too he had a head full of plans for the days ahead. Like a man all fixed and permanent he was, though at the very time the air was full of our pleadings to the governor to take us away from here.

And whilst we worked, our eyes were ever on the lookout down the river for sight of Lord Delaware's ships coming with plentiful supplies which Sir Thomas said the Company had been purposing to send in time. But one long day after another that fiery old sun come up out of the east, burnt on across the sky, and squenched its fearful scorching flames in the wide waters to the west again. [*Shaking his head.*] Ah Lord! And now after ten days a council meeting is being called aboard the governor's ship there secret and apart from the anxious people.

[*He moves on down the incline into the shadows. The light fades out and comes up on the right side stage.*]

Scene V

The captain's quarters on shipboard—a square porthole showing in the background between the curved ribs of the ship. Aloft in the night at the rear the faint outline of a mast with rigging shows—the scene below being like a cut-out in the side of the ship. A SAILOR *high up there on watch, motionless, is gazing off down the river. A rough table is in the center of the scene, with* SIR THOMAS GATES, *a crisp stern man of 50, presiding as governor. He has his hat on while the others are deferentially bareheaded. The members of the council in addition to Gates are* SIR GEORGE SOMERS, *a corpulent jovial gentleman of 60;* WILLIAM STRACHEY, 45; FRANCIS WEST, 24; *and others from former scenes—*PERCY, MARTIN, POWELL, NEWPORT *and* YEARDLEY. *Some of them are sitting, some standing. When the light comes up,* YEARDLEY *is up speaking vehemently.*

YEARDLEY. Our country needs us in a better cause. We have no right to take the lives of the women and children entrusted to our care.

MARTIN. [*Sitting with his chin on his stick.*] Mistress Yeardley.

YEARDLEY. True. And I would take my wife away from the horrors of starvation she has suffered, and the others likewise. Gentlemen, we all have served our king and country on many a battlefield and spreading sea. We stand ready as always to yield up our lives if need be. I know that. But the need is not here. It is too late.

TWO OR THREE VOICES. Hear, hear!

YEARDLEY. [*Warmly.*] We have only enough food to last us three weeks more at best. You have just heard Governor Gates say so. [*Indicating* GATES.] There is still time to get away to the fishing grounds in the north and home to England. This enterprise has failed.

MARTIN. Nay!

GATES. You hear John Martin's voice. Captain Percy, you too have been here from the beginning. You have governed this settlement. What do you advise?

PERCY. My voice is with Captain Yeardley's. I know naught else to do. We must give over this settlement.

GATES. Captain Newport.

NEWPORT. I have crossed the seas these several times in service to the colony. I have labored and hoped and prayed that it might not fail. If I saw one single chance of its continuance, I would say take that chance. But I see none.

[MARTIN *climbs shakily to his feet, leaning on his stick.* ROLFE *comes in at the left and stops in the edge of the scene,* AUSTIN COOMS *behind him.*]

GATES. [*Irritatedly.*] Yes, John Martin.

THE FOUNDERS

MARTIN. I was commander of the good ship Benjamin with Sir Francis Drake at Roanoke Island. And there I saw Ralph Lane and a hundred men desert their posts, calling for relief, crying "Take us away, we are starving here"—a hundred cowardly men. We took them away, and hardly had they left ere Sir Richard Grenville arrived with supplies. If they had but held on! [*A fit of coughing seizes him and he sits down.*]

SOMERS. You forget the Governor's report, John Martin. His majesty himself has forsworn us, given up his charter in this endeavor that has cost untold treasure in ships and money and men, and no return. [*Looking about him.*] Though Captain Martin's voice be brave, his enfeebled body calls loudly for succor from this death.

[*There is a nodding of heads.* ROLFE *steps quickly forward.*]

ROLFE. [*Saluting the governor.*] Captain Martin is right. Are we Englishmen or cowards, Sir George Somers? Shall the failure at Roanoke be repeated here? I say it shall not.

AUSTIN. [*Sturdily.*] And I agree.

GATES. [*Loudly, as he bangs the table.*] John Rolfe, you are not a member of this council, nor you, sirrah.

AUSTIN. [*Firing up.*] Sirrah?

VOICES. What means this rash intrusion? Dismiss them both. Out with them!

ROLFE. [*Saluting again.*] But I am one of the colony, and as such I should have a voice.

AUSTIN. [*Testily.*] We are Englishmen and there is warrant for having our voices.

GATES. [*Loudly.*] Then should the rabble all have voices, and authority, leadership, would be lost.

MARTIN. John Rolfe is here at my invitation. As a member of this council I have that privilege. Let him speak.

POWELL. I call for the council vote. The hour grows late.

VOICES. Vote, vote.

GATES. Captain Martin claims his right. We must grant it.

[*To* ROLFE *as he salutes again.*]

Cease thy saluting then, John Rolfe, and speak to the point.

ROLFE. Do we have faith in God, faith in ourselves, faith in the rightness of our cause? If so we will not give up this colony.

AUSTIN. Nay, we will not. We will yet find gold.

GATES. [*To* AUSTIN.] Silence!

PERCY. We have faith, but no food.

SOMERS. What good is faith to a dead man?

[*Some of the* COUNCILORS *manage a laugh.*]

GATES. We have no time to listen to your preachings tonight, Master Rolfe. [*He rises.*]

ROLFE. [*His eyes blazing.*] Then ye will all prove traitors!

[*A few of the council are stung at this. Mutterings rise among them.*]

THE FOUNDERS

SOMERS. Dost thou call me a traitor? [*Feeling for his sword.*] By heaven—

[AUSTIN *jumps forward to* ROLFE's *defense, then turns spasmodically back before* SIR GEORGE's *gleaming weapon.*]

ROLFE. I fear not thy sword, Sir George. 'Tis the first defense of weakness. [*Righteously.*] I am a man of peace.

GATES. [*Pushing* SOMERS *back in his seat and watching* ROLFE *narrowly.*] Let him speak!

ROLFE. In my soul I believe the Almighty still watches over us.

GATES. Oh—yes, yes. [ROLFE *salutes again.* GATES *in exasperation strikes the table with both his hands.*]

ROLFE. The king has given up the old charter? Then let him. For now the Virginia Company itself will make our laws and supply us as is said in the new charter his excellency—[*Indicating* GATES.]—has brought. There are men in that Company in London—men who watch for our interest, who will never cease in their care for us—Sir Edwin Sandys, the Ferrars, Southampton, and the noble Sir Walter Raleigh himself—they are determined that we found here in this new world a more liberal government, a newer, better England—plant it whether the king will or no, a government of free Englishmen.

AUSTIN. [*Applauding.*] Hear! Hear!

VOICES. We will not listen to these treasonable mouthings.

[*With the exception of* GATES *and* MARTIN, *they are all on their feet now.*]

ROLFE. [*Loudly.*] I am loyal to my sovereign, but I am loyal first to this colony.

VOICES. Enough, enough! The vote, your excellency!

ROLFE. [*His words tumbling on.*] Why have we been brought to this hour of failure and weakness? I'll tell you—because we have made enemies of the Indian people here and not friends. If they were our friends they would feed us.

STRACHEY. But they are not our friends.

ROLFE. They could be if we would persuade them. They have food. They are numerous. They know the ways of the wilderness. They could teach us many things. With them as our friends Jamestown would thrive. And we could help them. Fear, fear, hate and killings have been between us. We say we would live in peace with them if they would let us. They say they would live in peace with us if we would let them. We say they hate us. They say we hate them. And thus through the years they have confined us here, crippled and weak. And through the years we have filled their villages with the lamentation of death from our guns. They are waiting for the hand of friendship—waiting!

SOMERS. Give them that hand and as they hold it they will brain you with the other.

ROLFE. Pocahontas says they yearn for peace. She is our friend. I believe her.

GATES. Aye, we have noted her yearning for white flesh—

ROLFE. [*His eyes blazing.*] Sir!

GATES.—Alone of all her people—a most strange and un-normal appetite! Proceed.

ROLFE. [*Restraining his anger.*] Her strangely gentle heart deplores this spilling of blood between us. Not only that, but in her quick thinking she sees that her people are ignorant and poor beside us. Give them tools and they could build homes, clear fields and become a people of strength and pride. Yes, in time they could be taught from our books, be taught our blessed Bible. And all of us together working in a common cause— we would go on to triumph here. [*Clapping his hands together like a street exhorter.*] Oh, gentlemen, think of all this heathen nation waiting for our uplifting hand, waiting for our true religion to liberate their benighted souls—even as it was our aim to do.

PERCY. We are thinking of them and have been these three years.

ROLFE. [*Saluting.*] Sir, I have a plan—

GATES. [*Yelling.*] Cease thy saluting!

ROLFE. Aye, sir. [*He starts to salute again and stops himself.*]

VOICES. He has a plan.

GATES. [*Snapping.*] What is it?

ROLFE. Captain Smith made the Indians promises. Others have made promises, and they have not been kept. Let me go to them with axes, hoes, saws, adzes— instruments of peace—and say to them—these are yours. We give them to you freely. We will teach you to use them—help you to build yourselves good homes and clear your fields.

POWELL. What they want is guns—to murder us with.

ROLFE. There is the rub, gentlemen—as it says in the

play—guns with which to kill one another. I will give them no guns. I will carry none. I will go as a Christian brother.

PERCY. And get your throat cut.

ROLFE. And prove to them our kind intent. As Pocahontas says, we have offended them deeply. This was their land first. They think we have come to take it away from them. But there is much land here—a vast stretch from sea to sea—enough for a multitude of generations to come.

GATES. Nay, this is our land alone. We have a patent for it.

ROLFE. And who gave us that patent? The king. And who gave him his right to it? No one. Like the Spaniard he claimed it because he thought he had the power to —out of the void and in his pride of emperor he claimed it. Power!

AUSTIN. [*From the rear.*] True, true.

SOMERS. [*Angrily.*] By right of exploration—Cabot, Gilbert, Raleigh, Drake—

ROLFE. [*Hurrying on.*] A struggle between two powers then. And the Indian is winning. You are met here to decide the giving up this fort. You let the Indian win. You leave him in his barbarity and his heathen condition. You slink away home—and to what sort of welcome, I ask you? Not as heroes will you come and with flags of welcome flying. Nay, but as men who have failed.

AUSTIN. And with no gold.

ROLFE. The king and parliament, the Virginia Company, all England herself will condemn you for it, and your names will not shine on the page of history. Give me a few men to carry these gifts to the Indians in exchange for corn and game—[*He starts to salute again, the bows to* GATES.] You have heard me, Governor Gates? What is your pleasure, sir?

GATES. My pleasure would be to cut away thy loose tongue. But even so, gentlemen, there may be some reason in his words.

[ROLFE *beams.*]

MARTIN. Let us try Master Rolfe's advice this once. [*Loudly.*] I say so.

GATES. [*Slapping the table.*] I give thee two days to return, Master Rolfe. Captain Percy and I will choose the men to go with thee.

ROLFE. [*Saluting.*] And unarmed.

GATES. Unarmed. [*Shouting.*] Get out!

ROLFE. [*Happily.*] Yes sir. [*He turns and goes away followed by* AUSTIN. *The council murmurs.*]

POWELL. But certain, your excellency, you will not send innocent men off to be butchered in cold blood.

PERCY. We can spare John Rolfe but no good man.

GATES. [*Glancing about to see that* ROLFE *is out of hearing.*] Nay, I am not so great a fool, Captain Powell. You and Sergeant Abbot shall follow with soldiers through the woods to protect them. Goodnight, gentlemen.

[*The* COUNCILORS *put on their hats and turn to leave. The scene fades out. There is a moment of darkness, and then from the forest up at the left the signal whistle of an Indian is heard. Other whistlings answer it. A drum begins to beat in the distance. The light comes up on the woodland stage at the left.*]

Scene VI

In the forest near Jamestown. The war-painted OPECANCANOUGH *and his son* KO-COUM *are revealed standing under a tree on the upper level on watch. Two or three* WARRIORS *are seen peering out through the undergrowth at the back.* OPECANCANOUGH *throws up his hand in a warning gesture.* KOCOUM *points off. The drum beats more loudly. The two watchers stand listening a moment and then glide away into the shadows, the* WARRIORS *following. The drum continues beating an instant and then dies. From off at the right toward the fort the sound of men's singing is heard, and* JOHN ROLFE *and his little band of men enter, marching up the incline toward the forest. Among them are* TODKILL, GARRET, LOVE, SCOT, *and two young fellows in their middle teens,* THOMAS SAVAGE *and* HENRY SPELMAN. *They are carrying hoes, rakes, axes, mattocks, a box of trinkets, and a big iron pot slung on a pole as gifts to the Indians.* ROLFE *at the head of the procession carries a piggin in one hand and a rake with a white cloth on it held aloft in the other. His spirits are merry now over his pious undertaking and he is singing away with some of the others joining in.* TODKILL *is silent and keeping a sharp lookout about him as he goes.*

ROLFE AND MEN.
>Cold's the wind and wet the rain,
>>Saint Hugh be our good speed.
>Ill is the weather that brings no gain,
>>Nor helps good hearts in need.
>>>Hey down a down, hey down a down,
>>>Hey derry derry down a down.
>>>>Ho! Well done,
>>>>To me let come,
>>>Ring compass, gentle joy.

>Troll the bowl, the nut-brown bowl,
>>And here, kind mate, to thee!
>Let's sing a dirge for Saint Hugh's soul,
>>And down it merrily.
>>>Hey down a down, hey down a down—

[*They go on into the leafy woods, their song receding. A medley of yells and shriekings breaks out as the Indians set upon them from their ambush. The drum begins to pound again. The yelling and shrieking continue, and* ROLFE'S MEN *come pouring back in a rout, leaving their tools and gifts in the hands of the attackers,* ROLFE *coming last. He is wildly waving his flag and crying out half-hysterically toward the woods.*]

ROLFE. Friends! We are your friends! Chesk chammay! Chesk chammay!

[TODKILL *and* SCOT *grab him.*]

TODKILL. Back, you fool! Back. You'll get us all killed!

[*They rush him on down the incline toward the fort.* POWELL *and* ABBOT *with a small troop of* SOLDIERS, *among whom are* LAYDON, JOHNSON, WHITE, WEBB, BARRET, DODS *and* BRINTON, *dash by and tear on up into the woods. They attack the* INDIANS, *and through the trees we see the flashes of gunfire and a hand-to-hand struggle in the swirling smoke. The* INDIANS *are finally driven off, the soldiers pursuing them with halloos and intermittent firings on into the distance. The drum dies and the scene slowly fades out. The organ reprises a few bars of the "Saint Hugh" song, and then from the darkness of the center stage a trumpet blows and the voice of* GEORGE YEARDLEY *is heard calling.*]

YEARDLEY. Hear ye! Hear ye! people of Jamestown!

[*The light comes up on the rear of the center stage.*]

Scene VII

The interior of the dilapidated fort, with the center portion in darkness. CAPTAIN YEARDLEY *and* THOMAS SAVAGE, *the boy trumpeter, are standing aloft on the watchman's walk, their figures illuminated in the light.* YEARDLEY *wears his sword belted on and holds a paper in his hand. From the shadows below comes the murmur of the gathering people.* YEARDLEY *lifts the paper and reads in a running, announcing voice.*

YEARDLEY. This the seventh day of June in the year of our Lord sixteen hundred and ten! Whereas in the infinite mercy of God the hour has come when we must forevermore yield up this colony in Virginia, it is expressly commanded and ordered by his excellency the governor, Sir Thomas Gates, that each and every one of us shall depart these confines in all humility of soul and contriteness of heart. Let there be no unseemly behavior, no loud and boisterous tongues, no rejoicing in this solemn hour. And whereas it is rumored that certain rebellious spirits have threatened the firing and destruction of this fort on our leaving, it is further ordered and commanded as law civil, military and divine, that whosoever shall damage one palisado or one plank or lift his hand in harm to any piece, part or parcel thereof, shall do so—[*With harsh emphasis.*]—on pain of death! This ruined and desolate habitation will remain a monument to those who gave their lives for this vain endeavor until the wilderness from which we hewed it forth doth claim it back again. [*He folds up the paper.*] Let the flag be lowered—for the last time. [*He removes his hat and stands at attention.* SAVAGE *sounds the solemn mournful call for the lowering of the flag. Unseen hands from below let the flag rapidly down. As it goes out of sight,* SAVAGE *stops his blowing.* YEARDLEY *puts on his hat again and calls out.*] Gather at your respective posts and wait the beating of the drum!

[*He and* SAVAGE *go down the ramp at the left behind the church, and the light fades, rising slowly and full on the center stage. A number of* COLONISTS *are already assembled there, and others are coming in. Some are seen in the court of guard building and the cabin getting their last-minute belongings together. There is a general movement of preparation for leaving. Most of the people have little bundles in their hands, and some wear old pieces of sailcloth or shawls to cover their heads and shoulders. A few of them walk with strength and resolution, but most of them weakly and tremblingly along, here and there helping one another arm in arm. There is an obvious though quiet elation in their emaciated forms. They keep stirring restlessly about. In the broad light of day we see that the fort is dilapidated indeed. Some of the roofs have holes in them and a wide section of the palisade itself is fallen down—beyond which* LOVE *is walking on guard.*]

ANNE. [*Her baby* VIRGINIA *in her arms, her husband* JOHN *by her side.*] 'Tis a blessed dream—we are going home at last.

VOICES. [*Fervently, almost whisperingly.*] Home—home!

READ. [*Drooped under his sailcloth like a gaunt sick bird.*] And may we never wake from this dream in this cursed land again.

VOICES. Amen to that.

[*Others come in from the right and left. The* REVEREND RICHARD BUCK, *30, a slender pale-faced young cleric, enters on the upper level by the church, walking with the aid of a tall staff and with his bundle slung over his shoulder. He kneels down by the little cemetery plot in silent prayer.*]

ANNE. My baby will live now.

[LAYDON *pats her shoulder comfortingly.* LUCY FOREST *in ragged widow's weeds, calls out.*]

LUCY. We'll have food at the fishing grounds.

VOICES. [*With almost a groan.*] Food, food.

[AUSTIN *comes in from the left with his cane and tattered droopy-plumed hat. He is accompanied by* PHARAOH *with a little bundle.*]

AUSTIN. [*Satirically.*] What a brave sight is this, ye goodly people!

VOICES. We are content, we're going home.

OTHER VOICES. [*Echoing.*] Home, home.

[AUSTIN *stands over at the right and* PHARAOH *with him.*]

AUSTIN. [*Angrily to* PHARAOH.] I mark your new obedience, Pharaoh, now we're going back to England.

PHARAOH. And I'll serve ye faithful there, Master.

READ. [*Managing a croaking laugh.*] Poor Sir Austin Cooms is sore at heart. For nary a grain of gold did he ever find here for all his searchings.

AUSTIN. Hah! Mock away, blacksmith. I yet would find it but for this base deserting.

[JONAS *enters at the left with little* MARTHA RAYNOR, *an emaciated girl about ten years old, in his arms.* BARBARA BLEWETT *is with him, carrying a large bundle.* JONAS *turns* MARTHA *over to* BARBARA *and* TEMPERANCE YEARDLEY *and goes back the way he came.*]

TEMPERANCE. Rest here, Martha. A little while and we'll be riding on the big ship and see the flying fishes and the white birds sailing by.

[*Little* MARTHA *sinks down on the bench by* TEMPERANCE *who begins stroking her forehead.* BARBARA *sits next to her, bowed over, one hand holding onto her bundle.*]

OLD EDWARD. [*With a shout as he holds up his cudgel.*] Look at that there walking stick. I got it from a crippled Indian that day with Master Phettiplace we was hunting for the iron mine. I broke in that Indian's brains, I did. I've gnawed the knob clean off. I keep a-chewing it. Cain't hinder myself. My gums is plumb full of splinters.

AUSTIN. [*Satirically.*] Try eating dirt awhile. Master Hunt done it in the year eight and he was dead 'fore cock crow.

READ. [*Imitating a rooster's crow.*] That cock—he flew off to old Powhatan. We couldn't ketch him.

[*Several* COLONIST YOUNG MEN *come in with their baggage and stand about the scene like the others. Little* MARTHA *suddenly begins calling in a high feverish voice.*]

MARTHA.
  New brooms, green brooms, will you buy any?
  Come maidens, come quickly, let me take a penny!

TEMPERANCE. Poor thing, she thinks she's back in London calling her wares.

LUCY. No wonder God has cursed this settlement, Mistress Yeardley—the Company catching pitiful little boys and girls like crippled starlings on the streets and shipping them here!

MARTHA. [*Singing.*]
    Tomorrow the fox will come to town,
        Peep, peep, peep—

[*Stretching her arms pleadingly in the air.*]

    I must desire you, neighbors all,
        To halloo the fox out of the hall,
    And cry as loud as you can call—
        Whoop, whoop, whoop, whoop, whoop.

AUSTIN. [*Mockingly.*] Whoop, whoop.

LUCY. Silence on thy evil tongue, Austin Cooms!

[MARTHA *slides down on the ground and lies still.* BUCK *rises from his prayer now and stands reading his Bible.*]

TEMPERANCE. [*Feeling* MARTHA's *forehead.*] One minute she's burning like fire and the next as cold as the waterdrops in the king's river there.

THE FOUNDERS

[*She lifts one of* MARTHA's *hands and begins chafing it.* ROLFE *comes in from the right rear with a bucket. He goes over to a little framed box at the front of the cabin at the right and sloshes water on some tiny green tobacco plants growing there.*]

OLD EDWARD. If John Rolfe ain't simple in his wits, then the bells of Saint Paul's be naught but Indian drums—him mooning over his tobacco in this parting hour!

[ROLFE *turns and goes out with his bucket the way he came.*]

LUCY. He says he still has faith that God will somehow save Jamestown. He was all night praying in the chapel there.

READ. Simple all right—but yesterday leading unarmed men into an ambush of Indians! They'd all a-been killed if Sergeant Abbot and the soldiers hadn't rescued 'em.

DODS. And him standing there in the woods with the tears of sorrow falling down and crying—"Friends, friends, we bring ye gifts! Friends!"

[GEORGE YEARDLEY *enters at the left accompanied by an armed* SOLDIER. *He goes about, looking at the people's baggage. Stopping by* TEMPERANCE *he bends down and kisses the top of her head.*]

YEARDLEY. Youth and beauty were meant to have their day, my darling—but not here. And we will have it together, you and I, back in England. [*She looks up at him with a wan smile.*]

TEMPERANCE. I would we could have had our life here.

[ROLFE *re-enters with more water for his plants.* YEARDLEY *moves on. He calls out irritatedly to* ROLFE.]

YEARDLEY. Mayhap the Indian maid, Pocahontas, will care for your tobacco plants after we leave, Master Rolfe.

ROLFE. [*Stiffly.*] And a cruel thing I call it, to steal away with no word to her.

YEARDLEY. 'Tis ordered that our going away be secret lest Opecancanough set upon us at the last moment.

ROLFE. And even now Pocahontas has gone to Patowomack to her uncle Japazaws to plead for food for us.

READ. And we'll be well away ere she returns.

[POWELL, ABBOT *and a small squad of* WORKMEN *carrying shovels enter from the left.*]

POWELL. [*Saluting.*] The cannon are all buried, Captain Yeardley.

YEARDLEY. Good, Captain Powell. You have but time to fetch your luggage. [POWELL, ABBOT *and the men hurry back out at the left rear.* JONAS *re-enters with his little bag of luggage and stands by* BARBARA. YEARDLEY *examines her bundle. He speaks to her sternly.*] You may not carry this aboard, Barbara Blewett. Only small baggage is allowed. [*He lifts out a large and showy farthingale.*] Put it back in your cabin.

BARBARA. [*Holding to it as she stands up.*] No, no, Captain Yeardley, please!

YEARDLEY. Put it back.

BARBARA. [*Staring at the dress, her voice rising in a kind of keen.*] My man gave me this dress that day he come home from the fair. And he held me up in his arms and kissed me on the mouth and told me the

THE FOUNDERS

great news—we were sailing for Virginiay. Big and strong he was till this evil wilderness stole his strength away and laid him in the ground there. [*Caressing the dress with her hand.*] And now it will hang on a nail in the cabin all alone, nobody to brush it, to feel it. And the nail will rust away in the days to come, the roof rot, and the rain pour in and wash all its pretty colors away—hanging there with the spiders and the rats to gnaw at it, the birds to tear it away piece by piece to build their nests in the thick thorn.

JONAS. [*Kindly.*] What must be, must be, Barbara.

[*In silent grief* BARBARA *goes out at the right.*]

YEARDLEY. [*Stopping by* JOHN *and* ANNE LAYDON.] Nor that cradle—leave it behind, John Laydon.

[LAYDON *reluctantly picks up a cradle by him and carries it over to the cabin at the left, then returns to* ANNE'S *side.* ROLFE *goes out at the right rear for his luggage. A muffled drum begins a slow rhythmic beat off at the left.* YEARDLEY *calls out.*]

Make way, make way. His excellency, the governor!

[*The people who are sitting rise weakly to their feet and straighten up, and all turn facing to the left.* SAVAGE *enters, carrying a flag, accompanied by* SPELMAN *who is beating a drum. Behind them comes* SIR THOMAS GATES, *the governor, his hat in his hand and his bald head glistening in the sun. With him are* SOMERS, PERCY, WEST, MARTIN *and* STRACHEY, *the last the secretary and recorder of the colony and carrying a huge record book. Then come two or three orderlies with the governor's luggage and after them* POWELL, ABBOT *and their men with their bundles.* GATES *leads the way on to the rear and stops.* BARBARA BLEWETT *re-enters from the right rear.*]

GATES. [*Gravely.*] And now we say farewell to this city and to these dead. [*Looking at the crosses.*] Farewell to thee—William Brewster, Thomas Gore, Bartholomew Gosnold, Thomas Studley, George Kendall, Matthew Scrivener, Richard Waldo, Peter Winne, Gabriel Archer, John Ratcliffe, Thomas Forest. Farewell to thee, most noble servant of God, Master Robert Hunt, and to all the humble dead.

PEOPLE. Farewell.

BUCK. [*Lifting up his hands.*] So do these dead rest in Christ Jesus, martyrs and witnesses to our cause that has perished here.

GATES. [*Loudly.*] To the ship!

[SPELMAN *strikes his drum, and the people start on out.* TEMPERANCE *reaches down to lift little* MARTHA *to her feet and then gives a high shuddering cry.*]

TEMPERANCE. The child is dead!

[*Some of the people turn back.* JONAS *runs over and drops down by* MARTHA. *The drum is suddenly silent.*]

GATES. [*Somewhat harshly as he slams on his hat.*] Bear her body aboard.

[JONAS *picks her up.*]

JONAS. [*Brokenly.*] Rest, child, rest. Jonas holds you safe in his arms.

GATES. She shall have proper burial in the deep waters.

ABBOT. [*Fiercely.*] Praise be to God, this hellish wilderness has claimed its last body from amongst us.

[*The people move on,* YEARDLEY *coming over to accompany* TEMPERANCE, *and* BARBARA *walking with* JONAS *and taking hold of one of* MARTHA's *little claw-like hands as she goes. The drum sounds again its muffled beat, and the organ strikes up the "Huguenot Battle Hymn" in solemn slow march time. The people, led by* BUCK, *sing as they march out.*]

BUCK AND PEOPLE.
> Blessed is he whose filthy stain
> The Lord with pardon doth make clean,
> > Whose fault well-hidden lieth.
> Blessed indeed to whom the Lord
> Imputes not sins to be abhorred,
> > Whose spirit falsehood flieth.

[*The marchers go on down the river bank toward the ship that waits unseen off there, the song continuing.*]

> Thus I pressed down with pain,
> Whether I silent did remain,
> > Or roared, my bones all wasted.
> For so both day and night did stand
> On wretched me thy heavy hand,
> > My life hot torments tasted.

[*The singing and the organ fade on down.* ROLFE *enters from the right with his bundle of luggage. He stands alone in the scene looking about him. Lifting his face, the tears streaming down his cheeks, he calls out with fervent anguish in the air.*]

ROLFE. I keep my living faith in thee, O God! I keep it still. [*Loudly and piteously.*] Thou wilt not let this colony die! O hear me!

[*He turns and hurries after the others. The organ con-*

tinues playing, as it were a lament to the empty desolate fort, the scene of so many frustrated hopes and broken hearts, of so much suffering and death. The light fades out except for a gentle illumination on the little cemetery crosses by the church. It holds for a moment, and then dies. The organ surges in with a reprise of a few bars of the hymn and is silent for an instant, and then from the forest up at the right the sound of POCAHONTAS' *voice is heard humming the melody of the Huguenot Hymn. The light comes up there. Followed by some five or six* MAIDS, POCAHONTAS *is seen coming down the incline. They are all carrying baskets of corn and fruits.* POCAHONTAS *stops and calls out joyously toward the fort.*]

POCAHONTAS. Ay-ee-looh! [*She waits, and no answer comes back. She calls again.*] Ay-ee-looh! [*Alarmed, she dashes down the incline toward the fort. The light dies out behind her and comes up on the center stage. She runs into the empty scene, and the* MAIDS *hurry in after her. She looks wildly about her, calling.*] Friends! My friends—Master Rolfe! Mistress Yeardley! [*She stands listening, then runs frantically out at the left, still calling.*] Master Rolfe! Master Rolfe!

[*The* MAIDS *set their baskets down and gather in a group over at the right center.* POCAHONTAS *reappears from behind the church on the higher level at the back. She dashes over to the right and out, and then immediately in again. The* MAIDS *point off toward the river.*]

MAIDS. [*In an excited gabble, declaring that the colonists are sailing away.*] Ireh uscoend! Tassentassis ireh uscoend!

POCAHONTAS. [*Fiercely.*] Mattah! No, no! [*The light*

THE FOUNDERS

comes up on the river beyond the fort, and there the colonist ship, framed in its mystic halo of illumination as before, is seen sailing down the river, moving diagonally from left to right on its way home. POCAHONTAS *darts up through the gap of fallen palisades and pulling off the bright scarf that binds her hair, she waves it wildly, shrieking out.*] Come back! Come back! [*She stares off broken-heartedly as the ship disappears around a bend in the river. Then she turns sorrowfully back into the scene. Looking at the church, she moves over to it, and seizing the rope which hangs down outside, begins ringing the bell furiously. The frightened* MAIDS *huddle together at the sound. She falls to her knees, weeping, bowing her head over and beating the earth with her hands. Her voice rises in a wail. With loud lamenting, she stretches her hands to the sky, singing a prayer to her god, the great spirit that lives beyond the sun, asking him to send back her lost friends.*] Ireh, ireh, wingan chesk chammay! Ireh oughrath maunumummaon camerowath! Ireh, ireh, nummawh! Miske, ahone mangoite! [*She puts her face in the dirt, and the* MAIDS *gaze at her sorrowfully and helplessly. She stretches her hands upward again, repeating her prayer. Suddenly she springs angrily to her feet, her fists clenched, her face defiant. Her god will not hear her. The* MAIDS *gasp in horror at her behavior. She starts into the church. This is too much for her* MAIDS. *They scurry up to her and try to stop her, crying out that she must not go into that dreadful place, for the evil god of the white man lives in there.*]

MAIDS. Mowchesoh, mowchesoh, riokosick!

POCAHONTAS. [*Her face lifted.*] I pray to the great God of my friends. He is good and will hear me.

[*She pushes them aside and goes into the church. The
MAIDS squeal in fear, and gathering up their baskets,
they flee back up the incline the way they came. The
light comes on in the church, and there as if through a
scrim we see* POCAHONTAS *kneeling in anguished prayer,
pleading with* JOHN ROLFE's *God to send the colonists
back. Her supplication continues. After a moment her
manner changes. The God of the white man is answering her. She cries out wildly and joyously, her face now
alight.*] He speaks to me—from the deep sky he speaks!
They will come back! Yes, yes! [*She rises and hurries
out of the church and through the gap in the palisades
at the rear. An instant she stops and gazes down the
wide river, then dashes away along the bank to the
right. The scene slowly fades out. The organ surges in
with a strong reprise of the hymn again, and the lights
come on in the amphitheatre.*]

INTERMISSION

PART TWO

Scene I

The organ begins the overture, summoning the people back into the amphitheatre. At first there is the strong and vibrant statement of the first part of J. Farmer's "Te Deum," which gives way to a sprightly rendering of the melody "Summer Is Icumen In." This passes into the tripping and gay "My Bonnie Lass" of Thomas Morley. The crash of a wild Indian war dance, with shrilling flutes and a heavy pounding drum follows. This continues for a moment, then the organ moves back into the latter part of the "Te Deum" and ends. The light comes up on the center stage.

The fort has been repaired and the palisades rebuilt. Standing on the walkway at the rear is SAVAGE *blowing his trumpet for the people to assemble. The* COLONISTS *are coming in from the right and the left—among them the few women of the former scene.* JOHN ROLFE *is on the upper level looking off.* PERCY *and* STRACHEY *enter from the left,* STRACHEY *carrying a short-staffed British flag.* PERCY *holds a document in his hand.* POWELL *comes marching a squad of nondescript* SOLDIERS *in at the left. They line up at attention. At the right front are* YEARDLEY, TEMPERANCE *and*

POCAHONTAS. JONAS *is standing with* BARBARA *nearby.* SAVAGE *ends his blowing and the rat-tat-tat of a drum is heard beyond the fort.*

ROLFE. [*In loud announcement.*] Sir Thomas Dale approaches!

[*He comes down and takes his place by* POCAHONTAS. SIR THOMAS DALE, *45, accompanied by his flag-bearer and drummer and a spick-and-span guard of some six or eight red-capped* SOLDIERS *from his ship and under the command of the trim* CAPTAIN EDWARD BREWSTER, *25, enters at the right rear. With him is* RALPH HAMOR, *27, the new secretary and recorder of the colony. The enthusiastic* ROLFE *leads the people in an unenthusiastic cheer. Too many governors have come and gone for them to get excited.*]

ROLFE AND THE PEOPLE. Cheers for our new governor! Cheers for Sir Thomas Dale!

[DALE *looks about him and acknowledges the welcome with a few lifted strokes of his sword. He is a big raw-boned bearded man, square-shouldered and muscular— a wide-walking man of usually stern countenance and flashing eye but now smiling and genial. There is in him something of fire and fury when aroused, a mixture of religious fanaticism and the spirit of the psalmist David—a volcano of energy and will, of somber brooding when anger seizes him or things are going against him, but with a sense of humor and spirit of fun in him also. He has come to match his strength against the wilderness and from his appearance and manner no one could be better fitted for it.*]

THE FOUNDERS

DALE. [*In a loud heavy voice.*] Greetings to you, my people of Virginia!

ROLFE. Greetings to you, sir.

VOICES. [*As the* WOMEN *curtsey and* STRACHEY *dips his flag.*] Greetings.

DALE. Captain Percy! And my fellow soldier of old, Captain George Yeardley!

YEARDLEY. [*Saluting.*] Welcome to Jamestown, sir.

PERCY. [*Bowing.*] Herewith, sir, in accordance with the orders of our Company I hand over my commission as deputy governor to you which I received from Lord Delaware at his leaving these two months by.

[DALE *takes the document and passes it on to* HAMOR. *Then he moves about among the people, looking at them and smiling. All watch him intently.*]

DALE. Once more the Virginia Company of London sends a new governor to lead the enterprise—I by my count being the twelfth in these four years. I am acquainted with the constant ruination of this colony. But yet I believe God watches over it—or else it would have perished long ere this.

ROLFE. [*Jubilantly.*] He does, he does.

DALE. [*His glance sweeping by* ROLFE.] Mark how a year ago when you were forced to yield up the fort and sail away from Jamestown—how Providence sent Lord Delaware in time, and like a miracle you met him in the river and were rescued. And before that, Governor Gates himself arrived in the starving time to share his food with you. Now I am come with supplies and a company of my own soldiers to make permanent and strong that which has been tottering and weak. I bring you greetings from your Company in London. [*He moves on.*] And I bring items of good news. Master John Rolfe's cask of tobacco which Lord Delaware bare home has found favor with the Company. I doubt not it will prove a commodity of much worth and in time we shall be able to supply a great market which now belongs to the Spanish merchants. Let Master Rolfe show himself.

[ROLFE *steps forward.*]

I commend you, Master Rolfe.

PEOPLE. John Rolfe! John Rolfe! [ROLFE *bows.*]

ROLFE. [*Calling out.*] I say all praise to the lady Pocahontas, your excellency, who taught me the curing of it. [*He turns, takes* POCAHONTAS *by the hand and leads her forward to present her to* DALE.]

PEOPLE. [*Cheering.*] Pocahontas! Pocahontas!

[DALE *takes off his hat and makes her a sweeping bow.*]

DALE. And the thanks of the Company and all of us to you, dear maid. Your goodness is known in all England.

ROLFE. I have taught her much in the Christian faith, sir. Already she reads from the New Testament and recites the commandments. [*He gestures to* POCAHONTAS *encouragingly.*]

POCAHONTAS. [*Hesitating, then speaking in a clear childish voice.*] Thou shalt have none other Gods before me. Thou shalt not—

DALE. Good. And hast thou catechized her?

ROLFE. Aye sir, and sounded her well on Bishop Bayly's "Practice of Piety."

DALE. [*Heartily.*] Very good!

ROLFE. And she awaits your order for baptizing.

DALE. And that she shall have. [*Apparently joyous.*] This news sits well to my heart. For with her in the fold of Christ, many of her benighted people will doubtless follow. [*There is a nodding of heads.*]

ROLFE. They will.

VOICES. Aye, aye.

[AUSTIN *now pushes himself forward.*]

AUSTIN. And greetings to you, your excellency. You know me, Sir Austin Cooms that was, but now poor Austin Cooms. I was wont to see you at the Mermaid Tavern in time agone.

DALE. [*Chuckling as he stares at him.*] Thou art much changed, Sir Austin.

AUSTIN. Aye, as all must be who bide long in this wilderness.

DALE. And for the better, I trust.

[*Some of the people laugh.* AUSTIN *looks about him.*]

And I have more news—for you lonely men. The Company promises to send a sampling of maids out in Captain Argall's ship to make ye wives.

[*There is a strong reaction of pleasure to this.*]

MEN'S VOICES. [*Calling out.*] Let 'em come soon. Wives, aye, that's what we need.

DALE. Fair and virtuous ones.

READ. Their virtue matters not so they be women.

[*The people laugh again.* DALE's *geniality now suddenly changes and he looks out at them, his voice harsh and emphatic.*]

DALE. I said God watches over us. But it is not what God will do but what we ourselves will do. Governors have come and gone here, colonists have come and died here.

PERCY. Yea, three out of every four.

DALE. You remain. Now I am determined to do what others before me have failed to do—to build this colony permanent and strong. And I shall be merciless as this task I have been set to do is merciless. [*His eyes gleaming out at them from under his shaggy brows.*] The Company has ordered me to win this final battle against the wilderness or leave my bones to rot here. I have accepted their command. And if I fail there will be no governor to succeed me. This land will be yielded over to the red man and to Spain. It hath already been decided so. But I shall not fail, and you will not fail. I stake my life upon it and I stake your lives upon it. Why after these four years is this colony still weak—why so few in numbers here? [*He walks among them again, his voice ringing out.*] Is it because of disease and hunger and cold and the ever-watchful Indians? I say nay. It is because of the wranglings and dissension of your former governors and their councils, and the cowardice and weakness of your own spirits. And where the spirit is weak the body is likewise weak. The hand of authority over you has not been strong

THE FOUNDERS

enough. Now it shall be. I am a soldier. I command men in battle. This is a battle then and I shall be your commander, and as I tell ye so shall ye do. [*He pulls a document from his pocket.*] The Company has issued new laws for your governing—no longer civil, political and divine, but martial laws.

[*A murmur arises among the people.*]

VOICES. Martial laws!

DALE. Aye, military laws, with the power of my soldiers and their guns behind them. They shall be posted in the marketplace for all to read. And each captain shall read them to his company. [DALE *stares at* PERCY, *a hard smile playing about his lips.* ROLFE *looks blankly about him then up at* DALE. *He starts to speak and is silent.* DALE'S *hardness seems suddenly to vanish, and he is genial again.*] Speak, Master Rolfe.

ROLFE. I—sir—these colonists have suffered much, your excellency. They already have had hard laws to obey. The laws of Sir Thomas Gates were hard.

DALE. And obeyed willy-nilly. Some have obeyed them—true, and some have not. Now all shall obey as they labor in a common cause for the Company.

ABBOT. [*Muttering.*] Aye, we labor for the Company.

[DALE *looks out at him as if kindly. He moves on among the people.*]

DALE. The Company that has still kept faith with you against all difficulty—noble gentlemen in England who have mortgaged their lives and property to hundreds of thousands of pounds in your behalf. [*Stopping by* ABBOT.] Your name?

ABBOT. Sergeant Jeffrey Abbot, sir. I was a common soldier in Ireland and the Low Country. [*He gazes at* DALE *with his unblinking icy eyes.*]

MARTIN. [*Stepping forward.*] And one of our bravest men, sir. He came to the colony in the first supply.

DALE. You say you labor for the Company.

ABBOT. And have these several years.

DALE. So do I labor for the Company. [*He smiles.*]

ABBOT. And never for ourselves. [*A little recklessly and yet pleadingly.*] And the fruits of our labor go into the common storehouse there—to be doled out equally, sir, whether a man labor little or much.

VOICES. Aye, aye.

MARTIN. [*A bit apologetically.*] He has been ill, your excellency. Twice he has lain at death's door with wounds from the savages. Captain Smith's wheelhorse man he was.

YEARDLEY. The council has pondered these complaints, waiting your coming, Sir Thomas.

DALE. [*Quietly.*] And well ye did wait.

ABBOT. The terms of my service long are up, sir. I was promised a bit of land at the ending thereof.

VOICES. We were. Yea, land for ourselves.

ROLFE. The chance to build their cabins, sir, have some private property of their own.

VOICES. Aye, aye.

ABBOT. [*Encouraged by the attitude of the others.*]

THE FOUNDERS

These shoes on my feet—full of holes they are—worn out as I work my guts away from light till dark. But can I get new ones? Nay, I must wait the day the cape merchant issues shoes to all. 'Tis not so with the councilors and the captains. They have their privileges.

DALE. [*Quietly.*] And rightly so as is their class.

ROLFE. We pray your excellency to take note of these things and help the men to their deserving.

ABBOT. We were promised our rights as Englishmen here. But we have no rights.

VOICES. True, true.

ABBOT. The clothes I wear? The Company's. The tools I work with?—the Company's. The corn we grow, the tobacco we plant?—all the Company's. I came here hoping to make a place for myself and a girl back in England. I beg you, sir, let me keep that hope.

[*The people are murmuring, and some of them now show alarm at* ABBOT's *bold words.*]

ROLFE. With each new governor, sir, the laws have grown harsher. I fear the Company does not understand our case here. I think, sir—

DALE. [*Suddenly yelling.*] You are not to think, Master John Rolfe! You are now a soldier. [*In loud and stern announcement, looking about him.*] The old promises are revoked by the Company in this document. [*He taps the paper in his hand. The murmurs and mutterings die down.*] And the services of every man shall continue in common till this struggle be won. It were madness otherwise. If each man were allowed to pursue his own private purpose and gain and pull his separate way, this colony would break to pieces in a week. Only as we are united can we be strong. [*He turns to* ABBOT.] As for thee, Sergeant Jeffrey Abbot, I will crop neither thy ears nor slit thy scurrilous tongue as they deserve this time. Nay for Captain Smith's memory and thy services in the Low Countries I will be lenient. [*Smiling, he reaches out and snatches away* ABBOT's *old faded and half-rotten insignia of rank and flicks it to the ground.*] Private Abbot, common soldier, ye be now, and ordered to double sentry watch and hard labor to suit my pleasure. Take him away.

[*He gestures to* CAPTAIN BREWSTER *who comes over with two* SOLDIERS, *and they march* ABBOT *up the incline at the right and into the darkness. The people gaze at one another in doleful uncertainty.*]

[DALE *moves up by the church with his sword drawn and turns to them.*]

You are all soldiers now. This document declares it. As soldiers shall ye work, shall march, shall lie down, shall attend chapel, shall eat and rest and do your necessary acts of nature—hear me—soldiers! And as commander I shall see to your obedience. [*His voice grows suddenly kind again and genial even as he smiles.*] In your minds I can hear you saying—the new governor is a hard man. So I am. You say the Company may not understand your case. I say it understands well enough. Therefore these new laws. Too many have been selfish, willing to go their own way, weak, spineless, filled with dismay and desolation heretofore even before they began their labor here. Then is it wondrous that death conquered ye? I say not. Listen to me. Look into my eyes. There is no fear here —not in me. Strength is here! [*He strikes his breast*

THE FOUNDERS

and draws back his shoulder.] Stand up, stand up. [*Almost yelling.*] You there, with bent shoulders, lift them!

[*Some of the people straighten up.*]

Aye, already strength is coming to you—like wine beginning to warm pallid blood. And ye shall grow stronger still. My will shall be your will, and in that will ye shall be unconquerable. Nothing will defeat you if the heart is strong to stand against it. The fevers, the flixes, the nightmares, the murdering savages, hunger nor heat nor cold can destroy you if you will them so not to destroy. For thus you are armed against them. Heretofore this colony has waited for gray and gluttonous death to come creeping out of these swamps to carry you to the vile and wormfilled grave. [*Cutting the air with his sword.*] Nay, we shall march boldly to meet him—to the sound of the trumpet and the drum—march with concerted steps—one for all and all for one! And we shall conquer here! Let us cry with one voice. Loudly let us cry! Long live Jamestown! [*With his sword he directs the cheer.*]

VOICES. [*Led by* ROLFE.] Long live Jamestown!

DALE. [*Yelling.*] Louder, stronger!

VOICES. [*More loudly.*] Long live Jamestown!

DALE. Every soul! You, Martin! Percy! Strachey! Women—all!

ALL. Long live Jamestown!

[DALE *laughs and lowers his sword.*]

DALE. [*More quietly.*] And long live the Virginia Company and his majesty the king over it. Now to the ship for the unloading. Later I will organize the colony into its proper platoons and companies and with their respective leaders. [*Smiling out at them and bowing like a courtier.*] And the few dear ladies still amongst us here let them come along, for I have pots and pans and kitchenware aboard for their choosing—

[*The* WOMEN *show their thankfulness.*]

—and also much of women's gear, pretties and laces, ribbons and bolts of bright cloth and garment stuffs for their adorning.

[*The* WOMEN *applaud joyously.*]

And the princess Pocahontas for her baptizing will need a new dress to suit her beauty.

ANNE. [*Holding up her hand.*] And needles and pins, your honor? There be only this one old needle left on Jamestown Island.

DALE. Aye, dozens of new needles. [*Barking out his military command.*] Stand to attention!

[*The* PEOPLE *snap to attention as if with one will, staring at him with a mixture of fear and admiration.*]

And now we begin our work. And as we are strong we shall go forth in defiance of the Indians whom we fear not, building and planting and to find the riches of gold and silver and the great South Sea that waits beyond the mountains there. And we shall receive the praise and adulation of all England with—Well done, thou good and faithful servants. Let our hearts be joyful this day. Let our tongues sing—nay, not some doleful hymn—but a gay song to fit the occasion of this our fresh and happy beginning. [*He begins singing in a great soaring voice a sort of folk nonsense song, using his sword to beat time like a conductor, the organ joining in.*]

>As it fell on a holiday,
>   And upon a holy tide-a,
>John Dory bought him an ambling nag
>   To Paris for to ride-a.

[TEMPERANCE, YEARDLEY, ROLFE, BUCK *and others join in.*]

VOICES.

>To Paris for to ride-a
>And upon a holy tide.

DALE. March!

[*With his lifted sword, he leads the way to the right rear, all beginning to sing now and all marching in military formation.* BREWSTER *and one of the soldiers who have taken* ABBOT *off now re-enter and join their group.*]

DALE AND PEOPLE.

>The first man that John Dory did meet
>   Was good King John of France-a,
>John Dory could well of his courtesie,
>   But fell down in a trance-a.

VOICES.

>To Paris for to ride-a
>Upon a holy tide.

[*The people are now going out at the right rear, the song building, and some show of spirit obviously rising in them.* ROLFE *is walking with* POCAHONTAS *and* YEARDLEY *with* TEMPERANCE. *The last to go are the flagbearer and drummer.* JONAS *goes up the incline at the right.*]

ALL.

> The roaring cannons then were plied
> And dub-a-dub went the drum-a
> The braying trumpets loud they cried
> To courage both all and some-a—
>
> To Paris for to ride-a,
> And upon a holy tide.

[*They go out. The scene fades, and the light comes up on the woodland side stage at the right.* JONAS *is standing there with his musket.* ABBOT *is walking his post, coming out of the shadows and going back, a heavy pack on his back. One of* DALE's *soldiers stands motionless in the edge of the woods at the rear.*]

ABBOT. [*Stopping by* JONAS *and speaking bitterly.*] Let the Hebrew slaves make brick without straw now. The tyrant has come.

JONAS. [*Gesturing toward the red-capped soldier.*] Whist for mercy's sake. You want your tongue cut out?

ABBOT. Let his iron fist beat the others down till the ground swallow them all. But not me. I shall yet escape from this hellish land. Somehow I shall yet escape—and live. [JONAS *runs up and shakes him.*]

JONAS. One word of such talk come to the new governor's ears and you're a dead man.

ABBOT. I shall be secret. Secret—and deep as my hate of him and the Company is deep! And there will be others like me. [*He walks his post on into the shadows,*

THE FOUNDERS

the soldier following him. The scene fades out, and the organ surges in with a strong reprise of several bars of the "John Dory" song. There is an instant of darkness, and then a spotlight comes in on JONAS, *focusing on him as he comes down the incline toward the audience.*]

JONAS. [*Looking about him.*] Aye, a tyrant no doubt the new governor was. But they say there's good and bad under a tyrant. So it was our wranglings and dissensions and backbitings were put down, and never had the colony worked as it worked now—planting apple trees and mulberry trees and vines for grapes and a bigger crop than ever of corn and vegetables and tobacco, and clearing new fields and ditching and digging, hammering and sawing and building. And the women too—what few there were—were set to labor dressing thatch, working hemp and flax, cleaning the fish and drying them, pounding corn and beating barley. And they wove baskets now and mats like any Indian women. Pocahontas when she could, come and taught them how. From early morning light the voice of Sir Thomas Dale could be heard, shouting his orders and giving his calls—a fearful and mighty man, full of moods and tempers—but in one thing constant evermore—his intent to obey the orders of the Company and make the colony strong. Most of our sickness fled away, and the surgeons had to leave off their cuppings and bleedings. And the colony thrived—for a while it did. But as time passed and there was no ceasing from the slaving labor, people begun to fret under the governor's harsh rule, and poor Jeffrey Abbot was not single by hisself in the hidden bitterness and growing hate. Aye, he was a cruel man, Governor Dale, and flogged any laggard, and often helpless sick persons, without mercy. Once catching two Indians snooping about the fort, he cut off their right hands and sent them home to Opecancanough to take warning what would happen to him and his people if they kept proguing about our settlement.

And there were no gentlemen any more at Jamestown —only working soldiers and the officers over them.

[AUSTIN *comes marching down the incline carrying a broken-handled mattock. In appearance he is much the common workman now and walks with a slight twist in his back.*]

AUSTIN. Hup-hup-hup! One-two-one-two. Left foot— right foot.

JONAS. How goes the stump-digging, Austin Cooms?

AUSTIN. Well, and all together up, and all together down. Hup-hup. Like prizing the jaw teeth of the giant Polyphemus, it is. And that red-top soldier watching over me like a hawk.

JONAS. You must be almighty strong in your back to break your mattock there.

AUSTIN. Nay, Sergeant Pharaoh of the big muscles done it and then slipped it to me for mine. There's still a morsel of kindness in him for his old master. He sent me off to have it mended. And my back can get a rest. [*Grimacing.*] Ah—Sergeant Pharaoh Perkins! But then I am promised to be a corporal in two weeks or more.

[*From the darkness of the center stage the sound of girls' voices is heard singing.* AUSTIN *turns suddenly and begins to beam expectantly in that direction.* TEMPERANCE *and* BARBARA *come up the incline.* JONAS *smiles sweetly at* BARBARA *and she back at him.* TEMPERANCE *carries candlesticks and a broom and* BARBARA *a bucket and mop. They go on into the woods. Following them come four maids skipping along, carrying wild flowers, blankets, a bolster and pillows. They are led by* POLLY PACE, *a bouncing, bright-eyed young woman of 23 or so. The others are* THOMASINE UTLEY, CICELY JORDAN *and* ISABELLA PROCTOR, *all around 19 or 20. Coming last is a big-bosomed woman of 30 with flaming red hair, servant to* POLLY *and by her called* GOODY REDHEAD. *They are dressed in tucked-up gowns, smocks and bonnets, and are singing in a round as they come.*]

GIRLS.
>Summer is icumen in,
>Loudly sing cuckoo.
>Groweth seed and bloweth mead,
>And spring'th the wood now.
>Sing cuckoo.

[AUSTIN *pulls off his old hat and bows to them, and* JONAS *nods and grins.*]

AUSTIN. Greetings, pretty Polly, greetings.

[*They dance around* JONAS *and* AUSTIN, *and the latter reaches out to touch them. But they elude his hungry hands and go on.*]

GIRLS.
>Ewe bleateth after lamb,
>Loweth after calf the cow,
>Bullock starteth, buck to fern go'th,

Merry sing cuckoo—
Cuckoo, cuckoo.

[*With the exception of* GOODY, *who stops by* AUSTIN, *they twirl on up the incline into the woods.*]

Well sing'st thou cuckoo,
Nor cease thou never now.

GOODY. How beest thy poor back, Master Cooms?

AUSTIN. [*Gazing off ecstatically and pointing.*] Angel of light and joy she be—and where her little feet touch the earth heavenly flowers should spring.

GOODY. [*Sharply.*] Who?

AUSTIN. Thy mistress, pretty Polly Pace.

GOODY. And if flowers did spring, she'd blister 'em like a killing frost with her tongue.

POLLY. [*Calling.*] Goody—Goody Redhead!

GOODY. Coming, mistress. [*She flirts her smock at* AUSTIN *and goes on into the woods. He stands staring off.*]

JONAS. [*Looking out over the audience.*] Aye, for a while bitterness and fret are put away and all is great to-do at Jamestown now. Last week, after piteous months of waiting, ten of them—[*Gesturing behind him.*]—marriageable maids arrived, and there is big news too about Master Rolfe and Pocahontas—nay, Rebecca she is now. She was baptized in the church this March month—Master Rolfe give her that name Rebecca—helpmeet of the Lord—and now he is ready to give her his own name. They're fixing up a room for 'em in the blockhouse there for the wedding night.

[TEMPERANCE *calls from the distance.*]

TEMPERANCE. Come help unlock the inner door, Jonas!

[JONAS *goes into the wood.* AUSTIN *starts to follow, but* JONAS *gestures him back. He stands fanning himself with his old hat.*]

AUSTIN. [*Gleefully.*] Such a pursuing and such a courting that's been going on. The very air is full of perfume and women's sweet prattle. Such chatter and whisperings coming out of their quarters at night. Such looking in the glasses too—and snipping and sewing and pinning and unpinning, forming and conforming. Such a stir with sticks and combs, cascanets, dressings and purls—and falls and squares, busks, bodies and scarves—rabatoes and borders, tires, fans, puffs, ruffs, cuffs, muffs, fusles, partlets, frislets, bandlets, fillets, crosslets—and such la-la-ings over girdles, farthingales and kirtles—

[JONAS *returns down the incline.*]

—like the madness of the seven peddlers' shops back in Sturbridge fair it is. [*Slapping himself and pantomiming.*] And their breasts they embusk up on high, and their round roseate buds they lay forth, and show at their hands there is fruit to be hoped. The men are all run crazy.

JONAS. Mercy, thy mind is full of bawdiness, Austin Cooms.

AUSTIN. Yea, I confess it. [*His hand at his back.*] 'Tis on women and women only these two days and nights. All thought of worthless gold is gone from me.

JONAS. Be thankful for that. But your talk was always of hating women.

AUSTIN. Aye, but that was ere she landed here. [*He gestures toward the rear.*]

JONAS. Polly Pace?

AUSTIN. Back in England I knew her and her eyes were all for me, but in my gentleman's high station I disdained her. Now 'tis different. This is a land of change. I shall accept her.

JONAS. Aye, she is a joyous thing. Hope well for her choosing thee.

AUSTIN. [*Jubilantly.*] And I give over all former oaths and claims of bliss of bachelor state for her sweet sake.

[*He picks up his mattock and goes down the incline. From the blockhouse off-scene comes the sound of the girls singing their song again.* JONAS *starts whistling it. The light fades from him. The organ surges in with a strong announcement of J. Farmer's "Te Deum" and continues. The light comes up on the center stage.*]

Scene II

Interior of the fort. A festive setting. The church has been pushed in and is facing toward the center. We see into its foreshortened interior as if the front wall were off. At the upper rear is the altar with its snow-white gleaming cloth and set with numerous tall lighted candles. Other candles are burning from holders on the walls. Behind the altar is a stained-glass window with the light streaming through. The court of guard building and the cabin are pushed off scene, now that the point of view of the spectator has been changed. In the shadows at the back the line of palisades shows beyond the church. The church is decorated with flowers and greenery—wild easter lilies, dogwood sprays, redbud, azalea, bayberry, pine boughs and cedar. When the light comes up some thirty or forty COLONISTS *are gathered in front of the church, winging off to each side. A procession of women, led by* SAVAGE *dressed as a choir boy and carrying a crozier, enters from the right. The first in the procession are* BARBARA, ANNE, *and* LUCY. *They are followed by the group of marriageable maids. All are wearing their best finery for the occasion, and carry bouquets of violets and woodpinks. A procession of men enters at the left front meeting them, led by* HENRY SPELMAN *carrying a British flag. Behind him come* MARTIN, POWELL, HAMOR, BREWSTER *and others. The two processions turn and move up toward the church.* BUCK *in his clericals enters from the left rear, goes into the church, kneels an instant before the altar, then turns and stands facing out, his Bible in his hand. The organ strengthens, and* ROLFE, *accompanied by* YEARDLEY, *enters from the upper left and goes into the church. The two stand just below* BUCK, *waiting.* ROLFE *is all diked out in new doublet and hose, and his hair is brushed and combed. A murmur of excitement runs among the people and they all stare off at the right front. The organ strengthens again in an announcement. Little* VIRGINIA LAYDON, *five years old, enters, dropping flowers from a basket she carries on her arm.* POCAHONTAS *in her bridal attire comes behind her, accompanied by her uncle* OPACHISCO, *a grave stout chieftain of some 60 or more, imposing in his feathers, beads, copper ornaments and embroidered deerskin cloak, and by* TEMPERANCE. *Next comes* GOVERNOR DALE *in his red coat and finery.* POCAHONTAS' *two brothers,* PATAPSCO *and* NANTAQUAS, *clean-limbed young warriors of 21 or 22, are with him. Little* VIRGINIA *leads the way on up toward the church. When she gets near the steps,* ANNE, *her mother, reaches out, takes her hand, assists her on up and then stands with her to one side. Then others*

move up and take their places. GOVERNOR
DALE *with gestures assures the now hesitating* OPACHISCO *that the temple of the white
man's God is safe for him. The chief is disturbed by all the goings-on.* ROLFE *steps out
and meets* POCAHONTAS *in front of the altar.*
YEARDLEY *moves back. The people begin singing, the organ accompanying.*

PEOPLE. [*With* TEMPERANCE *leading.*]
>We praise thee God, we knowledge thee
>>The only Lord to be.
>And as eternal Father all
>>The earth doth worship thee.

[ROLFE *and* POCAHONTAS *kneel down in front of* BUCK.
The organ and singing continue loudly, and OPACHISCO
*puts his fingers in his ears an instant to protect him
from the barbaric noise. The two young warriors gaze
stolidly at their sister.* BUCK *is now leaning down and
speaking to* ROLFE *and* POCAHONTAS *as the singing goes
on.*]

>To thee all angels cry, the heav'ns
>>And all the power therein,
>To thee cherub and seraphim
>>To cry they do not lin.—Amen.

BUCK. [*To* JOHN ROLFE.] Wilt thou, John, have this woman to thy wedded wife, to live together after God's ordinance in the holy estate of matrimony?

ROLFE. I will.

BUCK. Wilt thou, Rebecca, have this man to thy wedded husband, to live together after God's ordinance in the holy estate of matrimony?

POCAHONTAS. I will.

BUCK. Who giveth this woman to be married unto this man? [*He looks over at* OPACHISCO.]

DALE. [*Touching* OPACHISCO's *arm and prompting him.*] Give—you give. [*He points to* POCAHONTAS *and then to* ROLFE. OPACHISCO *nods his agreement.*] Her uncle, Chief Opachisco and her two brothers who stand in place of her ailing father, Powhatan. [BUCK *puts* POCAHONTAS' *hand in* ROLFE's.]

BUCK. I, John Rolfe, take thee Rebecca to my wedded wife—to have and to hold from this day forward—

[*The scene fades slowly down to half-dim as he goes on, and the organ softens almost to silence. The people freeze in a motionless tableau. The sound of an Indian drum begins in the darkness up in the forest at the left. The light comes on there, revealing* OPECANCANOUGH, *his son* KOCOUM *and a number of* WARRIORS *looking down toward the center stage. Behind them stands their fearful okie, with* RAWHUNT *shaking his gourds vehemently in front of it. A basket is resting on the ground nearby.* KOCOUM *steps out and with a snarl slashes the air with his tomahawk in hate against the scene below.* OPECANCANOUGH *turns and they all kneel in supplication before the idol. The light fades out as the drum dies and rises full again on the center stage. The scene is energized to life once more.* BUCK *is holding out his hands over the kneeling couple.*]

Send thy blessings upon these thy servants, this man and this woman and may they ever remain in perfect love and peace together and live according unto thy laws. Amen.

PEOPLE. Amen.

THE FOUNDERS

[ROLFE *and* POCAHONTAS *rise and join right hands.*]

BUCK. Those whom God hath joined together, let no man put asunder. [*Looking out and addressing the people.*] Forasmuch as John and Rebecca have consented together in holy wedlock and have witnessed the same before God and this company and thereto have given and pledged their troth either to other, I pronounce that they are man and wife together. In the name of the Father, of the Son and of the Holy Ghost. Amen.

PEOPLE. Amen.

[ROLFE *kisses* POCAHONTAS. OPACHISCO *starts forward with a squeal of horror, but* DALE *grabs his arm.*]

OPACHISCO. [*Crying out his objection.*] Mattah! Mattah!

DALE. [*With a laugh as he pats his arm placatingly.*] It is the barbaric custom of the white man. [*He makes a smacking sound with his lips, and the people laugh. The organ strikes up a madrigal tune as the bride and groom come down the steps, and the* GIRLS *and some of the* MEN *run up and surround them in a clamor of congratulations, some of the women kissing* POCAHONTAS, *touching her hand and the men clapping* ROLFE *on the back.*]

VOICES. [*Ad lib.*] Blessings on ye! May you be happy forevermore. We love you, Pocahontas. You are beautiful. Blessings on John Rolfe. Hooray for John Rolfe!

[DALE *lifts his hands, and the people grow quiet. The organ softens down.*]

DALE. [*Loudly, jubilantly.*] In the symbol of this wedding we mark a new day for Jamestown. By her devotion and her love attested in this union our Pocahontas—now our beloved Rebecca—has brought peace between us and her people. Her father Powhatan has so declared and sworn it in a treaty and ordered his brother Opecancanough to cease his hates and maraudings.

VOICES. Good news, good news. Blessed be God for that!

DALE. Aye, blessed be God and blessed be these two. For now we shall no longer be threatened and hindered here. We shall spread our work abroad, come and go freely, plant our roots more deeply and widely. [*Sternly and warningly.*] But hard days still lie ahead of us, hard days. Yet we shall endure them, for success is certain in the end. And at this jovial hour of love think not upon the hardships we must face. Music!

[*The organ starts up loudly in a dance tune and then suddenly snarls into a confused discord. The people look apprehensively about. The light brightens on the woods up at the left, revealing* OPECANCANOUGH *and his group who have risen.*]

OPECANCANOUGH. [*Calling.*] Yee-yah! Ay-ooh!

VOICES. [*In alarm.*] There! See there! Opecancanough!

[*Some of the* SOLDIERS *start forward to seize their guns, but* DALE *gestures them back. A few of the people move toward the rear.*]

OPECANCANOUGH. [*Calling again, saying he has a marriage gift for* POCAHONTAS.] Thaig wenumm eraan, Pocahontas.

VOICES. What does he want?

THE FOUNDERS

DALE. What is it, John Rolfe?

ROLFE. The medicine man brings a wedding gift to Rebecca.

[*The people murmur their pleasure at the news.* DALE *beckons, and* KOCOUM *and* RAWHUNT *come down the incline into the scene,* RAWHUNT *carrying the basket. He sets it down, pulls his dark cloak up over his eyes, making mystic gestures in the air toward* POCAHONTAS, *then runs back up the incline.* KOCOUM *spits across in front of* POCAHONTAS. *She starts and puts out her hand pleadingly. He turns and marches after* RAWHUNT, *and follows his father and the others into the forest. The light dies out there.* DALE *moves over toward the basket.* OPACHISCO *hurries in front of him, pantomiming that this is bad medicine and for him not to touch it.*]

VOICES. What is it?

[POCAHONTAS *comes resolutely forward.* DALE *throws off the lid of the basket and lifts out a bundled dark skin. He unrolls it and holds it up. It is about four or five feet square and set in the middle with a crude but fearsome death's head. As he turns to show it to* OPACHISCO *and the two Indian youths, they wheel with a yell and go charging out at the left.* ROLFE *steps over and stands by* POCAHONTAS. *She is trembling and staring at the skin.*]

POCAHONTAS. The Indian curse my uncle Opecancanough sends to me. He says the Great Spirit is angry with me—[*Controlling the tremor in her voice.*]—says I will die—far from my people.

DALE. [*Laughing.*] Nay, have no fear of this vile superstition.

VOICES. No, no. You are safe with us, Pocahontas. No harm can befall you.

POCAHONTAS. [*Lifting her face.*] I do not fear. In Jesus I believe like my husband. I am baptized.

ROLFE. Our God will keep you safe.

[*She looks up into* ROLFE's *face, then turning takes the skin, throws it on the ground and puts her foot on it. The people applaud.*]

DALE. Take it away—burn it. [*A* SOLDIER *bears the skin and basket away.*] Music! Music!

OTHER VOICES. Dance! Dance!

[*The organ sounds forth again, and the people go circling around* ROLFE *and* POCAHONTAS *in a sort of children's singing game, some cutting dance steps as they go.*]

PEOPLE.

>My bonny lass she smileth,
>When she my heart beguileth,
>Fa la la la la la la,
>Fa la la la la la la.
>Smile less, dear love, therefore,
>And you shall love me more—
>Fa la la la la la la la la,
>Fa la la la la la la.
>
>When she her sweet eyes turneth,
>Oh how my heart it burneth—
>Fa la etc.
>Dear love, call in their light
>Or else you'll burn me quite—
>Fa la etc.

[*The organ now gushes up in a swirl of notes and changes into the dance tune of "Nancie." There is a scramble for partners.* AUSTIN *with his cane stuck under his arm is seen pursuing* POLLY PACE. *He gets her by the hand and holds on. With a laugh she gives in to him. And so they all pair off almost instantly—*DALE *with the widow* LUCY FOREST, YEARDLEY *with* TEMPERANCE, JONAS *with* BARBARA, *and so on.* ROLFE *and* POCAHONTAS *stand in the middle of the scene, and the dance swirls about them. A table of drinks and food is pushed in at the right, and those not dancing move over to it, among them the minister* BUCK. *While the dance is going on, a guard detail marches in from the left front and crosses the scene going up the right incline into the darkness.* ABBOT *is one of the detail, his face set and hard. The dance finishes with clapping of hands and merry individual turnings. The organ sounds a salute, and* DALE *steps out in front of the church. One of his red-topped soldiers runs in from the left with a wooden bowl in his hand, and the people all turn to the governor now.*]

DALE. Let the maids stand forth for their choosing. [*The group of brightly dressed girls led by* POLLY PACE *gather at the right.*] And those who hope to be husbands stand.

[*A whole swarm of colonist men almost run over one another grouping themselves to the left facing the girls.* AUSTIN *and* PHARAOH *are scrouging in the forefront.*]

A further augury of the permanence of this settlement is the coming of these maids to share their young lives with the men of their choice. Have ye marked your husbands? [*He indicates the bowl which the soldier holds.*]

GIRLS. [*In unison.*] Yes, your excellency.

GOODY REDHEAD. I can't write, but my heart knows. I done made my mark. [*The people laugh.*]

DALE. [*Sternly.*] Ye men who are to be disappointed take it not too much in grief. Other damsels will yet arrive. And ye lucky ones restrain your passion. No kissing, no fondling now. At the proper time our Reverend Master Buck will unite ye all in the church here.

AUSTIN. [*Calling out.*] Let it be tonight, your honor.

GIRLS AND MEN. [*In chorus.*] Aye, aye! Yes, yes. We can't wait.

DALE. Nay, ye must wait. The banns must be read first, even as in England.

[*He gestures to* POCAHONTAS *and laughingly she draws slips of paper out of the bowl in succession. The men wait breathlessly.*]

Thomasine Utley chooses—William Garret!

[GARRET *runs out to meet* THOMASINE, *and they stand happily side by side. One or two of the men show their disappointment.*]

Cicely Jordan chooses—Thomas Barret.

[BARRET *too runs out to meet his love. Again the same reaction on the part of one or two men.*]

Isabella Proctor—James Read. [DALE *continues to call out the names with dramatic and slow effect, and the people react joyously or not, as the case may be, at the pairing off.*] Joan Flinton—Edward Gurganey—Avis Glover—Thomas Webb—Chloe Holland—John

Dods—Barbara Blewett chooses—Jonas Profit! [*There is loud applause at this announcement, and* JONAS *smiles bashfully as he steps out, and takes* BARBARA'S *hand.*] Hester Morrison—William Spence—Drusilla Wright—Thomas Dowse—And Mistress Polly Pace chooses—[*He waits, and the people murmur.* AUSTIN *steps expectantly forward.*]

AUSTIN. I have already laid my heart at her feet, your honor.

DALE. Mistress Polly Pace chooses—um—Pharaoh Perkins.

[*The stout* PHARAOH *runs out to meet* POLLY. *She flings her impetuous arms around him and stands beaming by him.* PHARAOH *grins and looks about.* AUSTIN *stands horror-struck. A number of the disappointed men fling down their caps angrily against the ground, and some turn away out of the scene to the left. The people clap their hands.*]

AUSTIN. [*Shouting furiously.*] It shall not be, your honor! Declare it so! Nay, nay.

DALE. Silence, Austin Cooms. [*Looking at the slip of paper he has drawn.*] Be of good cheer, you are not forgot. Goody Redhead—ah—chooses Austin Cooms!

[*The people shout with laughter, and* GOODY *makes for* AUSTIN. *With a shriek he tries to dive away, but* LAYDON *and* OLD EDWARD *hold him.* GOODY *pounces upon him. He struggles against her, drawing back his cane to strike her.*]

GOODY. Good Austin, precious love.

AUSTIN. [*Yelling.*] Take thy claws off me, woman! [*He breaks loose from her and calls out fiercely.*] Is the world turned mad! The mistress there chooses my servant that was, and her servant chooses me, the master that was. I will not abide this harpy. Nay, I'll drown myself first in the king's river there.

DALE. [*Laughing.*] We do not compel thee to take her. But from her looks she could serve thee well.

GOODY. I could, Austin. I can sew and cook and know good home remedies for thy ailments.

POLLY. She does, Austin. Take her. There was Isaac back in England, a sickly man. And she made him well. Then Ephraim was down in his back like thee—she straightened him up, and Benjamin—she—

AUSTIN. [*Aghast.*] Merciful heavens, how many husbands has this woman had?

GOODY. They were my friends, Austin. My heart has been kept singly all these years for thee.

VOICES. [*Jocularly.*] Take her, Austin, take her.

AUSTIN. And what use have I for a woman now, and the heart broken in me this day in hopeless love? [*Turning and pointing his stick at* POLLY.] Not a wink have I slept these last nights thinking on thee and thy bright eyes and the singing music of thy voice. And now thou takest this low-life—this—this varlet for thy mate. Ah! [*He spits.*]

POLLY. [*Shrilly.*] Arrest him, your honor, tie him in the stocks for speaking so against my new husband—a big fine strong man can hold me light as a bird on one arm—and with great muscles hard like iron. Arrest him.

AUSTIN. And so thou hast been feeling of this Pharaoh with thy reaching hands—eigh? Thou loose woman!

[PHARAOH *springs at him.*]

Help, help!

[POWELL *and* YEARDLEY *grab* PHARAOH *and pull him back.*]

PHARAOH. He would blacken my wife's virtue!

[*A few titterings break out at this.* PHARAOH *glares about him.*]

DALE. [*Sternly.*] Restrain thyself, Pharaoh Perkins, or thou wilt cool thy leaping passion in the gaol house.

[PHARAOH *is released and returns angrily to* POLLY.]

And now we declare an end to these festivities.

DODS. [*Calling out a little timidly.*] Your excellency, we crave the indulgence of thy mercy.

DALE. Speak, private Dods.

DODS. [*In confusion.*] We would, sir—would have even one kiss, sir.

GIRLS. [*In eager unison.*] Yes, yes!

DALE. What does the minister say?

BUCK. [*Calling out from where he is standing near the table.*] Even so if it be uncommon brief, with no sin in it.

[DALE *breaks into a big laugh, and some of the people join in.*]

DALE. You heard the man of God.—No sin in it.

[*The couples kiss, some timorously, some with obvious ardor. A few of the kisses continue, and at a gesture from* DALE *the soldiers move in, separating these latter.* AUSTIN *has turned away with a groan at the sight of* POLLY *kissing* PHARAOH. DALE *calls out loudly.*]

Now all to your cabins—the men to their proper and separate quarters and the women to theirs! Captain Brewster, see that special sentries are placed. There is to be no slipping betwixt and between to unhallowed beds this night. As for Austin Cooms—Goody Redhead, I give thee leave to comfort him as best ye may. Soldiers, light Master Rolfe and his lady to their chamber and strengthen the guard across the big road. And a sweet rest to ye all.

[*The organ strikes up a reprise of the dance music. The women move out at the left and the men to the right. Torches are brought in by three or four soldiers, and* ROLFE *and* POCAHONTAS *are escorted up the incline into the darkness at the right, a number of the colonists bidding them goodnight in pantomime as they go.* DALE, YEARDLEY, TEMPERANCE, MARTIN, POWELL, BREWSTER *and* BUCK *go out at the right rear. Presently the scene is empty except for two or three soldiers pacing on sentry duty upon the higher level at the back and for* AUSTIN *who sits on a bench at the left front bowed over, his chin resting disconsolately on the knob of his cane. The scene fades down, and the light comes up on the right side stage. The soldiers with the torches are passing on into the shadows,* ROLFE *and* POCAHONTAS *remaining behind, standing side by side on the incline and looking out. His arm is around her.*]

ROLFE. Now after all these empty days and nights I

hold you in my arms, and there is no room for sorrow any more.

POCAHONTAS. [*Happily.*] Sorrow?

ROLFE. And loneliness. [*Looking up at the night sky and speaking fervently.*] Thanks be unto God who dwells beyond those stars—that he has guided me here to the work I was meant to do and the woman I was meant to wed. I feel my strength equal to this wilderness now. Your love makes me strong. It fills my heart with joy.

POCAHONTAS. [*Gaily.*] And my heart—feel it like a bird singing high in the tree. [*She puts his hand against her breast.*]

ROLFE. [*Drawing her to him.*] The days before I knew you now seem dead. The days ahead are full of light and wonder. For side by side and hand in hand we go to meet them. And here together we shall labor and build —your people and my people.

POCAHONTAS. Like you read me in the holy Book.

ROLFE. Aye. And whither thou goest I will go. [*Jubilantly.*] Clearer and clearer it has been coming to me— the vision of a great nation that will be, and we the founders thereof. And here our children will be born.

POCAHONTAS. [*Proudly.*] I am a strong girl, and I will bring many strong sons to you.

ROLFE. You will. [*He kisses her.*] And here in this new world they will live and work and grow. And justice and love and brotherhood shall be the charter over them and over their children's children down the stretch of time.

POCAHONTAS. And the tomahawk be buried now and the sword hang quiet on the wall? Yes?

ROLFE. Yes. And there will be peace in the land.

POCAHONTAS. [*Confidently.*] And no more the red blood of my people run into the dark ground.

ROLFE. Nay. For by our marriage we all swear friendship with your father and he with us.

POCAHONTAS. My father. He will keep his word. [*Looking off as if straining her gaze into the night.*] He sits in his long house. The wind of grieving blows upon him. The dead leaves of winter fall upon his heart. The black frost bites his gray head. He is old, and in the deep night the death song sounds from his lips. When the red sun burns in the east he stands up with a great cry—saying, where are my young men dead? Where is my daughter? I put my arms around him and sing to him—sleep, mighty father, king of great lands and rivers that run into the sea. [*Calling across the night.*] Sleep and rest, the moon of falling leaves comes not, the bitter cold and rain and snow be passed away! Sleep, sleep, my father, sleep. [*Shaking her head.*] I tell him there will be no more young men dead. I tell him so. Yes, yes, he says, Kiwasa—the great black spirit underground—sends evil dreams to me. I forget them. I give my hand to my white brothers, to my new son John Rolfe, in peace for my daughter's sake, I give it. My father will not break his word.

ROLFE. And with God's help the colony will not break theirs.

POCAHONTAS. Governor Dale is hard like the stone in the river falls. Teach him to be kind to my people.

ROLFE. We both must teach him.

[*She turns and gives him a quick little kiss on the lips, then with a sudden change of mood stares impishly up into his face.*]

POCAHONTAS. Why you love me?

ROLFE. Why?

POCAHONTAS. I know the why I love you. You make me feel safe—safe and happy with you. From the first day you do. And the sky is gray and the sun go gone when I don't see you. And my heart go bump-bump when you come, like the small Indian drum in the war dance. Always bump, bump. And when you touch me my cold hands be all warm—like in the gloves Barbara knit for me. See—now, now. [*She puts her hand against his cheek. He kisses it, and she gives a happy laugh.*] At first the people poke fingers at you. I see them. Master Rolfe loves the colored woman, they say.

ROLFE. But now they point no more.

POCAHONTAS. [*Teasingly.*] Why you love me?

ROLFE. Nay, I know not except I love you.

POCAHONTAS. [*Scoldingly.*] Mattah.

ROLFE. Yea then, because you are kind and gentle and no selfishness in you—always giving, giving your kindness and goodness to others, serving them, helping them. And sweet, sweet you are to my thinking beyond all measure—

[*She leans her head against his breast as he touches her hair.*]

—you with your happy laugh and bright and merry

ways—your tender hands—your—your hair and midnight eyes—all of you—body and soul. I love you—girl, girl of my heart.

POCAHONTAS. [*Murmuring.*] My husband.

ROLFE. At the first spell of you, I prayed and wrastled against it like a man against witchcraft, trying to forget you, to tear you out of my heart.

POCAHONTAS. [*Rapturously.*] You could not, you could not. My magic was strong.

ROLFE. Too strong. Aye, the nights I turned and tossed in my bed thinking of you—no rest, no sleep, thinking of you there across the way in Barbara's cabin, reaching out my hungry arms to you, my sinful arms. God forgive me.

POCAHONTAS. I knew, I knew. I came to your cabin at night to give you rest and love you. But your door was barred against me. Oh, oh!

ROLFE. And on the cold floor I spent my hours kneeling in prayer. And forgiveness came to me one morn with the breaking dawn—and with it love for you pure and undefiled—you my beloved wife this night.

[*With his arm around her, they turn up to the woods. Far away in the darkness a drum begins to beat.* POCAHONTAS *shivers and clings to* ROLFE.]

POCAHONTAS. The drum—in the forest—you hear it?

ROLFE. It is naught.

POCAHONTAS. My Uncle Opecancanough makes strong medicine for me with the witchman. [*Stoutly as she lifts her shoulders.*] You are more strong. I do not fear—with you I do not fear.

ROLFE. Yea, for God's grace is over you, my love around you.

POCAHONTAS. Your love—it will keep me safe—me safe with you, dear husband.

ROLFE. Always! You are cold, you tremble. Come, sweet wife.

[*They go on up into the darkness. The sound of the drum gradually dies away. The light fades out and comes up on the left front of the center stage again, revealing* AUSTIN *still sitting on his bench bowed over.* GOODY REDHEAD *is creeping up behind him. She puts her hands out and covers his eyes. He springs up, then clutches his back with a howl of pain.*]

AUSTIN. Yee-ay! [*He turns about the scene doubled to one side.*]

GOODY. Austin, love—

AUSTIN. Leave me, you cat from hell! [*He groans.*]

GOODY. Look at thy piteous condition, Austin. [*Pleadingly.*] I could help thee, ease thy pain.

AUSTIN. [*Lifting his stick.*] Stand back! Stand back or I'll brain ye.

GOODY. Please, Austin, please, my precious one.

AUSTIN. Don't precious me, or—

[*She suddenly grabs him and flings him to the ground, then jumps on his back with both feet. A crack is heard in the sound track as his joints snap together. He rolls on the ground like a man in a fit, shrieking.*]

You've killed me! My back is broke in twain!

GOODY. Nay, it is made well again. [*She hovers over him, then pulls him to his feet.*]

[*He slowly straightens up, turns about and finally feels himself.*]

Your muscle strings was all twisted together, Austin, I busted 'em loose. You heard 'em pop. You're healed now.

AUSTIN. [*Staring at her.*] I am? [*With a whoop.*] I'm cured! [*He trots about the scene and stops in front of her. She reaches out and takes his hand, smiling at him.*]

GOODY. And we'll walk together by the river now. The governor gives me leave to pleasure you, Austin. Look to his keep and comfort, he said. See the spangling stars above looking down with their tender light upon us two, on you and me. And the gentle dew all sparkling on the grass. Listen to me, Austin.

AUSTIN. [*Incredulously.*] Yea, I do.

GOODY. Aye, for love doth set my tongue aflame with words. Mark the little curling moon sinking down to sleep there beyond the cradling water—Austin, mark it.

AUSTIN. Aye, aye.

GOODY. [*Pulling him along.*] Come, we'll walk by the river. The soft wind is blowing and whispering in the trees, and the air's all heavy with the perfume of the bay bushes. The little waves go lap-lap among the gurgling sedges. Come, let's walk by the river, Austin.

AUSTIN. A little ways.

GOODY. A little ways is all I need.

[*They move out at the right rear,* AUSTIN *walking straight and spry. Just as they disappear, he claps his arm around her. The sentries continue silently pacing their beat at the rear keeping guard. The light begins to dim. In the distance off scene at the left* OLD EDWARD, *the night watchman, starts his sleepy call.*]

OLD EDWARD. Ten by the clock—and all is well! The night is fair—the air is sweet—[*He comes along in at the left rear with his pike and lantern.*]—and all is quiet in the city! God save his majesty the king—and all is peace at Jamestown!

[*He goes on into the darkness, his call receding in the distance. The scene fades out. The organ comes in with a reprise of the dance melody and dies, and the light rises on the woodland side stage at the right.*]

Scene III

JONAS *emerges from the forest rolling a wheelbarrow loaded with firewood, in the top of which a broadaxe is stuck. He is bundled up in an old coat against the cold. He comes on down the incline, stops his barrow to rest his game leg a bit, and blows on his hands.*

JONAS. [*Looking out at the audience.*] There's other husbands like me out gathering firewood this cold day to warm the cabins of their wives. Yea, I be married now to sweet Barbara, and I am much content—though some of the new-wed ones do share a shower of hot tongues, come day go night—as 'tis natural at first no doubt. The main thing is not to let it become a habit— as John Rolfe says. [*Chuckling.*] You must know that John Rolfe has a say-so for everything. Him and the Indian maid they be the most loving of people. The sun rises and sets in one for t'other. And such low sweet singing of her songs to him at night, and he reading the scriptures to her and teaching her—and the both of them together working at their everlasting tobacco, making it cure better and sweeter. Today cold as 'tis the two of 'em are out in the field there—[*Gesturing behind him.*]—digging and getting ready the plant bed for the spring—and she with a new baby to tend. Others are growing the weed—and babies too. Master Rolfe says mayhap this Virginia tobacco will turn out to be the real yellow gold we're looking for. Already there's a craving market for it beginning back in London.

Aye, things are some better here at Jamestown. I say some. There's peace with the Indians at last. And the governor is spreading the settlement—busy a-building a new city now called Henrico high on a healthy bluff up the river with good corn land paled in and watchtowers and a big church and a hospital for the sick. Later the colony will move up there, he says, and be safer from the threatening big Spanish ships.

He has put his bulldog, Captain Brewster, in charge there, the whilst he hisself has gone marching off with his soldiers and Indian scouts to the western mountains on another empty hunt for the gold mines and the great washing South Sea beyond. And the slavery keeps up—with "Heave away, my hearties, heave away at them heavy beams, swing the picks and mattocks, the hammer and the maul, and let the barrows roll." And I misdoubt not there's trouble brewing 'mongst some of the men up there—fellows like Jeffrey Abbot and Tom Webb—a mutiny to 'scape away to England in the pinnace, who knows. And over at the blacksmith and cooper shop too—[*He gestures across toward the left.*]—I've seen Tony Brooks and Humphrey Green and Rufe Price with whispers going betwixt 'em—a wink and a crook of the finger here, a nod of the head there—plotters all, I wager. And God help them if a hint of it ever comes to Governor Dale. [*From the direction of the fort a woman's voice calls.*]

VOICE. Jon-as!

JONAS. [*Answering.*] Yes, love—yes, my sweet. [*With a laugh.*] That's Barbara.

[*He grasps the handles of his wheelbarrow and goes down into the darkness. He has hardly disappeared when* AUSTIN *comes out of the forest puffing and blowing and bowed under a great bundle of wood tied with a bullace vine. The straight bonneted figure of* GOODY *walks behind. She carries a switch in her hand.* AUSTIN *stops on the incline and looks around at her, but she gestures him sharply on with the switch.*]

AUSTIN. [*With a vague glance up at the sky.*] Ah Lord!

[*They go on down into the darkness. The scene fades out, and the light rises on the side stage at the right, revealing the blacksmith and cooper shop. It is a rough planked shack, with a few barrels, pieces of lumber, staves and shavings showing about in the rear. We see into the shop as if the front wall were off. At the right are a bellows and forge with a fire going and an anvil in front, nearby a draw-horse, and behind it a grindstone and a small hogshead. When the light comes up, several men are working away and singing as they work—* RUFUS PRICE, *30, shaping a stave at the draw-horse with a drawing knife;* HUMPHREY GREEN, *28, hammering away on the anvil straightening out the red-hot snout of a pick;* JOSHUA SWIFT, *25, driving hoops around a cask at the right with a little maul; and* TIMOTHY PROCTOR, *26, at the grindstone sharpening a sword.* TONY BROOKS, *23, is sitting on a box over at the left mending the lock of a musket. Several other muskets are leaning against a saw-bench close by.*]

MEN. [*In a rough but pleasing four-part harmony.*]
    God prosper long our noble king,
        Our lives and safeties all;

> A woeful hunting once there did
> In Chevy Chase befall.
>
> To drive the deer with hound and horn
> Earl Percy took his way.
> The child may rue that is unborn
> The hunting of that day.

[GEORGE COTTON, *30, enters from the shadows at the rear. He carries a bucket of drinking water and gourd in one hand and a small sack in the other. The men look at him. He nods, and they stop working and gather around him apparently to drink.*]

PRICE. [*Quietly but intensely.*] All well at the storehouse?

COTTON. I'm in charge of it, ain't I?

PRICE. And the door will be unlocked?

COTTON. Unlocked and waiting.

[GREEN *dips up a gourdful of water and gulps it down.*]

PRICE. Shot and powder for the muskets there?

COTTON. Right here—plenty of it. [*He indicates the bag.*]

PRICE. Good.

[COTTON *goes to the rear and looks off.*]

GREEN. Drink, drink, but this water runs right through me, sweating at that there forge.

PRICE. The good sea breeze will soon cool you off.

GREEN. And the seagulls'll be cheeping around the masts singing sweet goodbye to Jamestown forevermore.

COTTON. [*Calling back.*] Ssh, not so loud.

BROOKS. And no more hearing them babies squalling there in the fort at night, thank God.

COTTON. There comes Captain Yeardley up from the tobacco fields. [*He turns into the scene and hurriedly hides the bag under the hogshead. The men scramble back to their work.*]

MEN. [*Singing again, COTTON joining in.*]
>   Lo yonder doth Earl Douglas come,
>   His men in armor bright,
>   Full twenty hundred Scottish spears,
>   All marching in our sight.

[YEARDLEY *enters from the right. The men salute him. He goes about examining things.*]

YEARDLEY. [*Pleasantly.*] I see you're still hard at it, men.

MEN. Yes sir, we are that. Work—work.

YEARDLEY. [*To* BROOKS.] The muskets mended?

BROOKS. Just finishing the last one, sir.

YEARDLEY. [*To* COTTON.] Return them tonight to the storehouse.

COTTON. Very good, sir.

[YEARDLEY *stands by the hogshead, his hand feeling it. The men are suddenly still, waiting.*]

YEARDLEY. [*Slapping the hogshead.*] We need a dozen of these for Henrico by the time the governor returns.

[*The men relax.*]

SWIFT. We have nine already, sir.

YEARDLEY. His excellency will be well pleased.

PRICE. And when do you expect the governor home from the mountains, Captain Yeardley.

YEARDLEY. He said he'd return after four weeks.

COTTON. And ye expect him to find gold, sir?

YEARDLEY. If it's to be found, Sir Thomas Dale will find it.

GREEN. [*Sanctimoniously.*] God grant it, then the colony will thrive.

YEARDLEY. The colony is thriving now.

PRICE. It is, it is.

GREEN. [*Wiggling the fingers of his great hammer hand in the air as if easing them.*] Aye, with hard labor a-plenty.

YEARDLEY. [*A little sharply.*] And right it should. Hard work and not gold will make this colony.

MEN. [*Quickly.*] Yes, sir. Aye. True, true, Captain Yeardley.

[YEARDLEY *stands an instant looking off. At a gesture from him the men return to their work. Then he goes back the way he came,* COTTON *accompanying him away a short distance, saluting, and then returning. The work of the men slows down again.*]

GREEN. A good man, Captain Yeardley. Would he were our governor.

PROCTOR. Aye, and Mistress Temperance our high lady with him.

PRICE. [*Roughly.*] It matters naught who's governor now. We will not be here.

BROOKS. If Abbot comes from Henrico the way you've planned.

PRICE. [*Correcting him.*] The way *we've* planned, *we've* planned. He'll be here tonight, I tell ye.

BROOKS. If he don't come—what then?

COTTON. Jeffrey Abbot will come if he has to kill somebody to get here. [*He lifts out the bag from the hogshead and hands it to* PRICE.]

GREEN. God forbid that! Then we might hang.

PRICE. We might hang anyway—if our plans miscarry.

BROOKS. [*Shuddering.*] No, no!

COTTON. Nothing to do but wait—work and wait. Load the muskets. I'll be ready at the storehouse.

[*He picks up the bucket and goes out at the rear.* PRICE *and* SWIFT *begin loading the muskets.* PRICE *leads off in the song again, and the labor is resumed.*]

MEN.
> Earl Douglas on his milk-white steed,
>   Most like a baron bold,
> Rode foremost of his company,
>   Whose armor shone like gold.
>
> Our English archers bent their bows—

[*The scene fades out, and the light comes up on the interior of the fort again.* GOODY COOMS, *with her frock tucked up, is washing at a wooden tub which is sitting on a stump below the church. A clothes-line running*

THE FOUNDERS

across from the court of guard building to the church is hung with an array of little babies' shirts, dresses and diapers. GOODY *is singing as she works energetically away.*]

GOODY.
>There was a jovial tinker,
>Who was a good ale drinker,
>He never was a shrinker,
>   Believe me, this is true.
>And he came from the Weald of Kent,
>When all his money was gone and spent,
>Which made him look like a Jackalent,
>   And Joan's ale is new.
>And Joan's ale is new, my boys,
>   And Joan's ale is new.

[*Several of the young wives begin coming out of their cabins and into the marketplace with their tiny squalling babies in their arms. The first to enter is* THOMASINE GARRET, *then* CICELY BARRET, *and after her* ISABELLA READ. *The young mothers are singing to quiet their offspring but not in unison, each carrying on her folk song to her own darling.*]

THE THREE.
>It was a maid of my countr-ee,
>As she came by a hawthorn tree,
>As full of flowers as might be seen.
>She marvelled to see the tree so green.
>At last she asked of this tree—
>How came this freshness unto thee,
>And ev'ry branch so fair and clean?
>I marvel to see thee grow so green.
>   The tree made answer by and by—

[GOODY *goes on with her song, mixing it in with the others'.*]

GOODY.

> The tinker he did settle,
> Most like a man of mettle,
> And vowed to pawn his kettle—
> Now mark what did ensue—

[JOAN GURGANEY *and* AVIS WEBB *enter with their babies. They are singing their own song too.*]

JOAN AND AVIS.

> Oaken leaves in the merry woods so wild,
> When will you grow green-a?
> Fairest maid and thou be with child,
> Lullaby mayst thou sing-a.
> Lulla, lullaby, lulla, lulla, lullaby,
> Lulaby mayst thou sing-a.

[*They all continue their songs, la-la-ing and swinging their infants about.* GOODY *bangs her washboard against the tub.*]

GOODY. [*Calling out shrilly.*] Why don't you take them brats to the river there and give 'em a good bathing like Mistress Rolfe told you—yea, you might drown 'em while you're at it. 'Twould hush their howling.

[*The young mothers toss their heads at her and begin to meet in the center of the scene to compare their jewels.*]

THOMASINE. [*To* CICELY.] Look how he grows!

CICELY. That he does. Soon he'll be heavy enough to take to the storehouse for weighing.

THOMASINE. My little Rebecca is the best baby alive. She never complains.

[*Little* REBECCA *lets out a sharp wail.*]

Now, precious, now lamby!

[CHLOE DODS *enters and begins showing her baby off.*]

CHLOE. I doubt his father will know our little John when he returns from Henrico.

[HESTER SPENCE, DRUSILLA DOWSE, *and lastly* POLLY PERKINS *enter with their infants. The squalling has set up in a fierce medley again, and the young women walk about swinging their tiny bundles.*]

GOODY. [*Yelling.*] Stop their almighty screeching! It drives me distracted! [*She washes away furiously.*]

POLLY. Wait till you have one of your own, Goody Cooms, and you won't talk like that. [*Some of the girls laugh.*]

DRUSILLA. How long is that to be, Goody?

GOODY. Now you just hush your mouth, Drusilla Dowse. Right now I'm washing your dirty little Sammy's safety clout. [*Putting her finger to her nose.*] Whew-w!

HESTER. [*Peeping at* POLLY'S *baby.*] Sweet, sweet, and his big, big eyes.

POLLY. The very image of his pappy. [*Nuzzling her face down to her bundle.*] Yes, you be, little Pharaoh!

GOODY. My Lord, why would a woman ever give a baby that ungodly name!

POLLY. It's a sweet name—even as my man is sweet.

GOODY. Well, love is blind, they say. [*Gesturing about her.*] But to look at this crop—it can see well enough —and in the dark at that.

[*The girls laugh. They gather in the center again, clucking and chucking and tickling one another's bundles. The squalling sets up once more, and the swinging goes on.*]

CHLOE. [*Calling into the air.*] When will our men come back to us! When?

VOICES. Aye, when—when!

POLLY. When the governor gets his new settlement built.

CICELY. And pray it be soon.

HESTER. Aye, and then we'll all move up there to Henrico and get out of these swamps and mosquitoes. My little Joseph here is bit slam to flinders.

AVIS. And my little Charity is too, with pimps all over her. And she was ailing all last night.

POLLY. Get Dr. Goodwin to give her some sassafras cordial. Little Pharaoh here just gobbles it.

AVIS. I keep thinking of my poor Tom Webb up there working, working like a slave at that Henrico.

CICELY. Work, work. I wager when they come home they'll all be skin and bones.

THOMASINE. And so weak they won't be worth a copper farthing. [*Several of them titter.*]

POLLY. My Pharaoh'll be strong a-plenty. He always is.

GOODY. [*Angrily.*] You and your man, Pharaoh! Yeah, and the first thing you know, Mistress Polly Perkins, you'll start having them pains again. And then you'll start that certain swelling and a-hollering for me at night to come and rub your stomach. Well, you can just let Pharaoh do the rubbing since he'll be the cause of it.

POLLY. You needn't be jealous, Goody. I'll let you help tend to all eight of my children one by one. [GOODY *throws up her hands.*]

THOMASINE. Aye, Goody was so wild over that old Austin Cooms, had to have him, just had to have him. Oh, Austin, sweet Austin!

[GOODY *marches toward her from the tub.*]

GOODY. [*Shaking her finger at her.*] I'll have you to know I married a man of high estate, Thomasine Garret—and by rights should be called Lady Cooms—a gentleman. And that's more'n you can say, any of ye. And he's a good man, good. [*She marches back to the tub.*]

THOMASINE. Oh yes, good, good!

POLLY. [*Calling off.*] Pocahontas! Come along, Pocahontas, the sun's going down!

CHLOE. That's what she's waiting for—the setting of the sun before she washes her little Thomas.

POLLY. It's some of that heathenism still in her.

GOODY. For shame, Polly Perkins.

POLLY. Well, I say true. Look how she ties the little fellow up on a board.

GOODY. Aye, to make him grow up straight.

CHLOE. Yistiddy when I come in her cabin there he was hanging on the wall like a string of beans or something.

GOODY. And as happy as a pea in a pod, I tell ye, whilst she done her housework like any good wife ought to. Her little Thomas never cries like your sp'iled critters, now does he?

CHLOE. And yistiddy in the early morning at the rising of the sun she tuk him to the river there and doused him deep under the cold water.

THOMASINE. That she did, and then she paddled him all over till his little yellow behind was red as a beet.

GOODY. To make his skin tough. Get on to the river with your younguns, all of you.

[POCAHONTAS *comes in with little* THOMAS. *He is wrapped up and tied to a board. She carries him in her hand by a looped cord. They all crowd around her. Laughing, she shows him pridefully off, holding him up high.*]

VOICES. [*Ad lib.*] Just see him! He's so precious! Chchk, chchk! Look at him. Look at Polly, Thomas. Look at Chloe. There—he's already smiling.

POCAHONTAS. He smiles, much he smiles. [*Glancing off at the setting sun.*] We go to the river now.

[*She leads the way out at the right rear. The others follow, all singing their variegated lullabies.* GOODY *stares after them, then begins wringing out more little garments and hanging them on the clothes line. Her song has died in her. Off at the right the voice of* AUSTIN *is heard.*]

AUSTIN. Hup—hup—one—one—two—one—two— [*He marches a work gang of some six or seven men down the right incline and into the scene.* JONAS *is in*

THE FOUNDERS

the lead with a gun. AUSTIN *also carries a gun. The others carry hoes and rakes.*] Halt! Ground arms! [*They do so in military precision.*] Count the tools in, Jonas Profit.

JONAS. Aye, Corporal Cooms. [*He salutes and* AUSTIN *salutes back.*]

AUSTIN. And you men, wash and clean yourselves for evening prayers. The ladies said there was a most unchristian smell of dirty bodies in the church last evening.

JONAS. March! [*The men march out at the left.*]

GOODY. Where are Captain Yeardley and Master Rolfe?

AUSTIN. They're in that tobacco patch together and will be till dark pinching at them worms. And such a crop! This time there ought to be enough to take away the market from Spain. Captain Yeardley'll be right along. How is Mistress Temperance?

GOODY. She's sitting there in her cabin waiting for her baby to be born. That starving time she went through causes it to be slower and harder than them other sassy things. [*She gestures toward the rear.*] So Dr. Goodwin says. But she'll come through safe, he says. She's strong and her spirit's tough—tough as Governor Dale hisself.

AUSTIN. [*Cutting his eye about.*] Then it's tough a-plenty. [*He comes over and appraises the row of baby clothes on the line.*] Well, we don't need any more colonists out of England for this settlement. We're providing plenty of 'em right here. [*Looking at her.*] Now I want to ask you something, woman.

GOODY. Aye, Austin.

AUSTIN. All these women—they're producing. Why be you not producing?

GOODY. Austin Cooms! For you to talk to me like that!

AUSTIN. You heard me.

GOODY. And now I ask you something, why ain't you producing?

AUSTIN. Me?

GOODY. You heard me. Them other men are producing.

AUSTIN. Ahm. [*Fanning himself irritatedly with his old hat.*] Why don't you let them women wash for their own babies? You've got enough to do to see after me.

GOODY. I crave to wash 'em, Austin, I crave to. [*She wipes the tears from her eyes.*]

AUSTIN. Now what ails ye?

GOODY. They laughed at me, Austin, them women laughed at me.

AUSTIN. You can't blame 'em for that, they're so proud of what they've been able to show forth.

GOODY. And they laughed at you, Austin.

AUSTIN. Hah!—[*Fiercely.*] Why the shameless hussies! They're all of menial blood, that's what.

[GOODY *bursts into tears and leans over the tub. He goes over and pats her shoulder. She turns on him furiously.*]

GOODY. I told you to eat of that snake root—Pocahontas recommended it. The other men et it. It has wondrous powers.

THE FOUNDERS

AUSTIN. Then I confess it to you. I've ate that stuff till I nigh foam at the mouth.

GOODY. Oh, Austin!

[BUCK *comes in at the left rear by the church.*]

BUCK. [*Calling down to them.*] To evening prayers, good people! Evening prayers.

[*He turns to the church and begins to ring the bell. The* COLONISTS *start coming in from different directions. The light fades down and out, and comes up after an instant of darkness on the blacksmith and cooper shop again.* PRICE *and three of his men, armed with muskets, are standing before the shop waiting. Some of them are giving their arms last-minute checkings. Off in the shadows at the right rear* PROCTOR *is standing on watch.*]

PRICE. All well?

GREEN. Dry and primed.

BROOKS. It's past time for Abbot. [*Calling softly to* PROCTOR.] How's the moon now?

PROCTOR. Resting like a boat down on the water— [*Chuckling.*]—ready to sail away.

SWIFT. Aye, sail away.

[*In the darkness the hoot of an owl is heard.* PRICE *cups his hand and answers.*]

PRICE. Whoo—ooh!

PROCTOR. It's Abbot, and Tom Webb's with him. [*He turns down quickly into the scene.*]

PRICE. Good.

[*They move over toward the right.* ABBOT *rushes in. He is ragged and wet from his great exertions. The men cluster around him.*]

Aye, we knowed you'd be here.

GREEN. How did it go off?

ABBOT. With murder and death, that's how. [*Hoarsely.*] Thank God, you've got the muskets. [*He gestures to the darkness and whistles.* WEBB *hurries in, ragged and wet also. He is given a gun, and* PRICE *hands* ABBOT *a sword.*]

PRICE. Tim Proctor here put a razor edge on it for you.

ABBOT. My thanks. [*He looks at the group.*] Each man knows his part.

VOICES. Aye, we know. We'll follow you.

ABBOT. We'll gather back of the fort—wait till all's asleep—then—[*He gestures with his sword.*] What of George Cotton?

PRICE. There at the storehouse—all set for springing.

ABBOT. Webb and I will take the sentry. You, Price, and the others make for the supplies—and then to the pinnace and away to England. Come on, men!

[*He lifts his sword, and they all steal off into the darkness at the rear. The light fades out and rises dimly on the center stage again. The fort is asleep, and the muffled figure of a sentry is seen standing guard on the upper level at the rear, leaning drowsily on his musket.* ABBOT *and his conspirators begin creeping in from the right rear, hidden from the sentry by the projection of the court of guard building.* COTTON, *the*

THE FOUNDERS

keeper of the storehouse, rises up out of the shadows by the building and beckons the men on. ABBOT *and* WEBB *steal across the scene along by the church. They suddenly spring out on the sentry, choke him silently to the ground, and* ABBOT *clubs him in the head with the butt of his musket. He lies crumpled and still.* PRICE *and the others have rushed across by the court of guard building to the storehouse just off scene and have begun bringing in bales and bags of supplies.* ABBOT *and* WEBB *run over and hurry them along.* ABBOT *starts to lead them back out at the right rear when a bugle sounds in that direction. They all stop in consternation.*]

PRICE. The governor!

ABBOT. [*Fiercely.*] By the north bulwark!

[*They dash up the right incline when a number of* DALE'S *red-topped soldiers, under the command of* POWELL, *come marching down to meet them. They turn headlong back.*]

POWELL. [*Yelling.*] Halt, halt!

[ABBOT *and his crew throw down their bags and bales and tear back across the center stage toward the left rear. In the distance at the left* CAPTAIN YEARDLEY'S *voice is heard calling.*]

YEARDLEY. The guard! Rouse the fort! The guard!

[*From different parts of the fort comes the babble of voices as the people are awakened from their sleep. Off at the right rear* DALE *is heard yelling.*]

DALE. What ho! Alarum, alarum!

[*A gun is fired off at the right, and the* MUTINEERS

flee behind the church. DALE *and his men burst in from the right rear, meeting* POWELL *and his men in the center of the stage.*]

POWELL. [*Shouting.*] They were escaping to the pinnace!

[DALE *leads the way toward the rear, pushing on behind the church with* POWELL *and the men to engage the conspirators hand-to-hand. A few more musket shots are heard from the darkness off at the left rear, then shouts and yells and the sounds of blows and scufflings.* YEARDLEY *and* ROLFE, *partly dressed, run in at the left,* YEARDLEY *carrying his sword and* ROLFE *a lighted lantern.*]

YEARDLEY. [*Gesturing to a few men dimly seen behind him.*] Man the gates!

[*The men hurry away in different directions.*]

DALE. [*Beyond the church.*] Surrender, surrender! I command ye to surrender!

[*People in their night clothes begin running in, among them* AUSTIN *in his old nightshirt and bonnet-like sleeping cap and* GOODY *in a ponderous sort of mother hubbard.*]

AUSTIN AND GOODY. What is it! What has happened?

VOICES. The Spaniards! The Spaniards!

OTHER VOICES. [*Horrified.*] The bloodthirsty Spaniards. At last they've found us. They will destroy us!

STILL OTHER VOICES. Nay, 'tis old Opecancanough and his warriors. They will murder us!

[*The babies are heard crying in different cabins.* DALE

re-enters from behind the church. At the sight of him the people are reassured.]

DALE. A most monstrous treason has been crushed.

[POWELL *and his soldiers come in from behind the church now, marching* ABBOT, PRICE, WEBB *and* COTTON *and their companions into the scene. They have been disarmed and some of them are bloody from the struggle. The sentry on the ground at the rear groans.*]

YEARDLEY. Look to him! [*He gestures and two soldiers run over and help the injured man off.*]

WEBB. Blessed be Christ we did not kill him!

DALE. So, Private Jeffrey Abbot, ye did not like the mattock nor the lash up at Henrico.

ABBOT. [*Hopelessly.*] God meant this so. Do what you will.

DALE. Well, and that I shall. And see thou likest the hangman's noose even less. [*To* POWELL.] Confine them in irons till the rising of the sun when just and proper execution shall be done upon them all.

PEOPLE. Lord have mercy! Lord have mercy on them!

[AVIS WEBB, *in her night clothes, rushes out from the crowd and clings to* WEBB, *weeping wildly.*]

AVIS. Tom! Tom!

[*She kisses him frantically.* YEARDLEY *and* ROLFE *sorrowfully pull her away, and* BARBARA *and* JONAS *help her sobbing off at the left.*]

DALE. [*Loudly.*] Set a double guard, Captain Yeardley. Away with them! [*The soldiers march the condemned men off at the left front, and* DALE *shouts out to the colony.*] Clear the market-place. Back to your cabins, people, every soul!

[*The people move on out and away in their different directions. In a moment the scene is empty save for a small number—the two or three soldiers at the back and* DALE, YEARDLEY, ROLFE, POWELL, HAMOR, *and* MARTIN *who has just come in leaning on his stick.* DALE'S *orderly has entered late at the right rear and stands to one side with a bundle on his back.* DALE *marches angrily back and forth.* BREWSTER, *with* LAYDON, READ *and* DODS, *comes in at the right center.* DALE *turns on* BREWSTER.]

'Fore the Lord in heaven, Captain Brewster, who can I trust? Aye, I shall get to the bottom of this, and woe to the men found wanting. You hear me, Captain Yeardley.

YEARDLEY. [*A little resentfully.*] The mutiny was with Abbot from Henrico—where Captain Brewster is in charge. Look to him, sir.

BREWSTER. In the dead of night Abbot and others rose up and slew one of our sentries, and he and Webb escaped. We followed fast.

DALE. We shall hear more of this in our quarters, Captain Brewster. Keep your men on duty about the fort, Captain Yeardley. And you, Captain Powell, tend to our soldiers, they have marched far from the hills.

YEARDLEY. And what of the gold mines, sir?

DALE. [*Angrily.*] Who speaks of gold mines this night? [*To one of his soldiers.*] Stand to my cabin there. [*To the* ORDERLY.] Prepare my bed. [*The* SOLDIER *and*

ORDERLY *salute and go out at the left front.* DALE *turns to* BREWSTER.] How goes the work at Henrico whilst I'm away?

BREWSTER. Well along, sir, with three streets of well-framed houses complete and the big brick church handsome to see.

DALE. Excellent. Good night, gentlemen.

[*They all salute, and he goes off at the left,* BREWSTER *with him. Under* YEARDLEY's *direction two soldiers go up and mount guard on the walkway at the rear.*]

ROLFE. God help Abbot and those poor men!

YEARDLEY. They will need it.

ROLFE. Captain Martin, your voice has authority with the governor. You will speak for them?

MARTIN. True, all should not be hanged.

ROLFE. [*Vehemently.*] We must stir the people, move them with one voice to cry out to the governor. We must. He may yet hearken.

YEARDLEY. Not Sir Thomas.

MARTIN. Best look to the safety of your own neck, John Rolfe. The colony needs you.

[*They turn and go away behind the church. The scene fades out. There is an instant of darkness and then the light comes up on the side stage at the left, revealing the interior of the governor's quarters—with a wall and a window at the back. A table and a few chairs are in the center.* DALE, *with his hat on, is standing to the left behind the table, and* MARTIN, YEARDLEY, POWELL,

HAMOR, WEST *and* ROLFE *are to the right with their hats off facing him.* BREWSTER *is standing in the rear. When the light comes up* DALE *is ending a stern reprimand to* ROLFE.]

DALE. And so I command you to silence, John Rolfe.

[ROLFE *who is seething with feeling controls himself and smokes his pipe furiously.* DALE *goes on loudly.*]

I took my sacred oath in England to uphold the laws of this colony. On the Holy Bible I put my hand. I kissed it with my lips, saying I would be true to my trust. And I shall. [*Crying out.*] And I shall, hear me! The earth grows red there in the east and these mutineers shall hang at the rising of the sun. Master Buck is even now preparing their souls for their eternal journey.

MARTIN. [*Strongly.*] I say let the leaders of this mutiny die, but not all.

DALE. All!

[ROLFE *clenches a frantic fist in the air.*]

YEARDLEY. Abbot served well here till this madness seized upon him.

ROLFE. [*Whirling toward* DALE, *his voice husky with pleading.*] And Tom Webb has a wife and little babe.

DALE. He should have remembered so ere this.

ROLFE. It was his aim to escape to England, then send for them, he says.

DALE. In an hour she will be a widow and the child an orphan.

THE FOUNDERS

MARTIN. But eight men, your excellency! As members of the council we feel we have a right to speak.

DALE. Under the military law, the council has been dissolved, and you know it, John Martin. This colony is now ruled by me as governor and lord high marshall. I speak the law, and I alone.

MARTIN. [*Sharply.*] And you should know, sir, that we protest this dictatorship.

ROLFE AND WEST. We do.

DALE. [*Staring at them astounded.*] How now, Captain Francis West? Do I find a mutiny among you gentlemen also!

WEST. Nay, you do not.

MARTIN. [*As WEST bows his head.*] We say let each separate case of these men be heard. Let justice be done to them lest the colony be further torn in its feelings and loyalties.

DALE. Justice is what they shall get, and I will take care of these feelings and loyalties.

ROLFE. [*Pushing forward and standing in front of DALE, his voice trembling with anger.*] You will take care of them, sir? You will give justice? Then I ask you for what purpose do we found this colony? I ask you.

DALE. And I will answer thy foolish question, Master Rolfe. We build it for the Company, for our king and parliament, for England, and for all Christendom against Spain and the Pope.

ROLFE. True, true. But first we build it for ourselves,

free Englishmen. Captain John Martin is right—this is a dictatorship and we have suffered enough under a harsh rule. The time has come to stop it. The people are growling and muttering against you, sir, and only these few rash ones have yet dared lift their arms in protest. But there will be others. And your Captain Brewster and his red-topped soldiers—

[BREWSTER *claps his hand on his sword, and* ROLFE *glaring over at him goes on.*]

—will not everlastingly keep us down. Look to it, sir, lest this colony rise up in righteous wrath and you have not eight in mutiny against you but two hundred.

[*He sticks his pipe back in his mouth and puffs away, staring straight at the governor.* DALE *gazes at him in silence an instant, then a smile begins playing around his lips.*]

DALE. Well by heaven, this puffing parson threatens me!

ROLFE. Nay I do not, sir. But I say we the people—we are this colony and our rights and our privileges should be looked to. During the night I have been from cabin to cabin and almost to a man and woman they beg your mercy for these condemned ones. Let not cruelty increase and bitterness amongst us. These poor men have suffered beyond belief. Sergeant Abbot was promised preferment that never came—promised rights he has never had—rights which were promised to all of us and which we have never had. And the girl he loved is dying in England.

DALE. [*Almost pleasantly.*] Nay, thou liest, John Rolfe. Did I not under Captain Martin's and Yeardley's and

THE FOUNDERS

thine own most constant persuasion give the farming class private gardens and three acres of land for hemp and flax?

BREWSTER. You did, sir.

ROLFE. Aye, and then you hauled the men off to labor at Henrico, and they have never enjoyed their land. Have mercy and save their lives.

DALE. [*Moving over toward* ROLFE *and stopping in front of him.*] You would have me break my solemn oath?

ROLFE. The Bible says, blessed are the merciful. An evil promise is not a promise, sir. We would have you remember the colony—not the Company, not England, not the parliament and king—but the colony, us, the people in this colony. And our voice is for mercy, and mercy let it be.

DALE. The people, the people!

ROLFE. Aye, their welfare, their wishes, their rights. If you commit this terrible killing, sir, your name—

DALE. [*With a shout.*] I know—will never brighten the pages of history! [*Yelling.*] Silence!

ROLFE. This is a new land here, our land. Here we are to live our lives. We have turned our eyes away from England and look to the future. And we know what we want here. We know what we need here. [*His voice soaring, his hands beating together.*] We want to be done with these harsh military laws. We want to make our own laws, to mete out our own punishment—and look to rules and orders of justice and life. Yea, we want the chance to govern ourselves—here—now—at Jamestown!

DALE. [*With a snarl.*] Thou art a traitor, John Rolfe. [*He suddenly seizes him by the throat and chokes him down to the table. With the exception of* POWELL *and* BREWSTER *the others crowd around in alarm.*]

VOICES. [*Ad lib.*] Your excellency! Pray, sir! Peace! Your excellency!

[DALE *half lifts* ROLFE *up and flings him from him. He stands glaring at him, his breath coming quick like a cat's in his boiling rage.* ROLFE *picks himself up and gazes at him with quivering face.*]

ROLFE. My arm is strong as yours, sir, but I will not raise it against you. The rightness of my words is stronger still.

DALE. Do not think, John Rolfe, because thee and thy tobacco have found great favor in England and thy marriage is well talked of by the queen, that thou art safe from my just anger. Nay, one more discharge of traitorous words from you, and so help me heaven, I shall with my knife mutilate thy wild tongue beyond all speaking. [*Yelling.*] Out of my sight! [*Seizing his sword.*] Out!

ROLFE. Very well, sir. [*Looking at the raised sword.*] 'Tis ever so—they that will not hear reason are quick to seize the sword.

[DALE *rushes at him, but* POWELL *and* BREWSTER *now step in front of him.*]

BREWSTER. Mark him not, your excellency.

[ROLFE *goes on out with some dignity.* DALE *looks after him with gleaming eyes, sits down and mops his face. Suddenly he laughs and strikes the table.*]

DALE. One of Christ's fools he is—[*Soberly.*] Aye—a dangerous fool with his doctrines.

MARTIN. There are many fools like him in this colony, Sir Thomas.

DALE. Yea, Captain Martin, I have noted thy liking for the sermon-spouting knave.

MARTIN. I believe him a good and honest man, and there is reason in his words.

DALE. No more of John Rolfe lest my stomach vomit. [*Looking at them, his anger apparently gone.*] Gentlemen, we have not yet won the victory for this colony. It is in sight, but not yet won. If rebellion is allowed to live it may still fail and all we've worked for wasted. Nay, the people shall receive their needed and final lesson now. [*Looking at* BREWSTER.] Speak, Captain Brewster.

BREWSTER. [*Saluting.*] In the Netherlands I should have said—all must die. Here I say—let the three leaders perish and the others suffer some easement from that penalty.

OTHERS. We agree.

DALE. Sound the trumpet, Captain Yeardley. Let the drum roll to summon the people. Captain Brewster, fetch the prisoners to the marketplace. [*Glancing up.*] The sun is rising. Pen and ink and the list, Ralph Hamor.

[*The men salute, put on their hats and go out at the rear.* HAMOR *brings a document forward with pen and ink and seats himself at the table.* DALE *begins to dictate.*]

Whereas mutiny and treason with murder most black and foul have been perpetrated against—

[*The scene fades out. In the darkness from the center stage the trumpet blows and the drum beats. The light comes up on the interior of the fort. Some thirty or forty* COLONISTS *have come in and others are arriving.* SAVAGE *is standing at the back blowing his trumpet, and* SPELMAN *is beside him sounding the roll of his drum.* DALE *and* HAMOR *come down the left incline,* DALE *with his drawn sword and* HAMOR *with a document in his hand. The people grow still. Some of the women are already weeping silently, their babies in their arms.* ROLFE, POCAHONTAS, JONAS *and* BARBARA *are in a group at the right.* YEARDLEY, MARTIN, POWELL *and* WEST *are at the left, and a number of young wives and husbands are in the center.* AUSTIN *and* GOODY *are with* AVIS WEBB *nearby at the right. Several of* DALE's *red-topped soldiers are stationed about the scene with their muskets ready for any emergency.* DALE *raises his sword, and the trumpet and drum are silent.*]

HAMOR. [*Lifting his document and reading in a strong, clear voice.*] Whereas mutiny and treason with murder most black and foul have been perpetrated against the welfare of this colony and the just laws of England and her king, and that there may be a sure and certain warning against their ever recurring hereinafter, I Sir Thomas Dale, by virtue of the power vested in me as governor and lord high marshall of Virginia, do hereby pronounce judgment upon the following men, to wit—Jeffrey Abbot, Thomas Webb—

[AVIS *moans and clings to* GOODY.]

—Rufus Price, George Cotton, Humphrey Green,

Joshua Swift, Anthony Brooks and Timothy Proctor.

[BREWSTER *and a number of his soldiers now march the condemned men in from the left. They are stripped to the waist and their hands tied behind them.* BUCK *follows after them with a Bible in his hand. He is intoning as he comes.*]

BUCK. Miserere mei, Deus, secundum magnam misericordiam tuam—

[AVIS *tries to get to* WEBB, *but* AUSTIN *and* GOODY *hold her back.*]

HAMOR. [*Continuing loudly.*] And whereas certain voices have been raised in their behalf that mercy and kindness be the mark of the Christian heart, the judgment against these each and several hereinbefore mentioned is remitted to a more honorable and happy leniency from hanging—

[*The people are relieved and show their pleasure at the news, though still anxious.*]

VOICES. Good, good. Thank God for the governor's mercy!

HAMOR. —to branding in the forehead with a red-hot iron and confinement at hard labor for one year—[*The people are jubilant, then are suddenly silent as* DALE *raises his hand.*]—save for Jeffrey Abbot, Rufus Price, George Cotton and Thomas Webb. They shall forthwith be taken to the dunghill outside the fort and there for their crimes and misdemeanors—be shot to death.

[*A great gusty groan goes up from the people, and* AVIS *screams.*]

AVIS. My husband! My husband!

[*She grows hysterical, and* AUSTIN *and* GOODY *try to quiet her. The people mill about, but the red-topped soldiers ring them in. The scene grows silent, the people staring in horrified fascination at the prisoners.* AVIS *falls weeping to the ground.* AUSTIN *and* GOODY *kneel by her.*]

AUSTIN. Nay, Avis, nay.

GOODY. Think of your baby, darling, your baby! [*They lift her up and help her away at the left.*]

WEBB. [*With a wild animal pleading.*] No, you won't do it! No! I won't let you kill me! No! [*He struggles and tries to break loose from the two soldiers who are holding him. They crush him to the ground, then pull him to his feet.*]

ABBOT. [*Calling over to* YEARDLEY.] This cross I wear, Captain Yeardley, I leave for my Mary in England I will never see.

[YEARDLEY *comes over and unfastens a little cross from around his neck.*]

YEARDLEY. It shall be sent to her, Sergeant Abbot.

[*At the reference to his former rank,* ABBOT *gives him a wan smile. Dark hoods are brought in by a soldier and are put over the heads of the four condemned men. The four that are to live are herded to one side.*]

BREWSTER. March!

[DALE *lifts his sword, and* SPELMAN *begins the mournful beating of his drum again.* SAVAGE *stands staring ahead of him, his silent trumpet gripped to his side.*

THE FOUNDERS

The eight men are accompanied off toward the right, BUCK *going along behind.*]

BUCK. [*Intoning as before.*] Amplius lava me ab iniquitate mea et a peccato meo munda me—quoniam iniquitatem meam ego cognosco—et peccatum meum contra—

[*His voice dies away as the men are marched out of sight.* DALE *stops at the extreme right and stands with lifted sword. The drum continues to roll.* ROLFE *turns his face away and holds* POCAHONTAS *to him, her head against his breast. In the distance* BREWSTER *is heard giving his command.*]

BREWSTER. Halt!

[SPELMAN *stops beating the drum and looks fixedly up at the sky. The people kneel, some of them hiding their faces, some moaning, and others gazing off at the dreadful spectacle.*]

DALE. [*Loudly.*] Ready—aim—fire!

[*A burst of gunfire follows. A gasp of horror breaks from the throats of the people.*]

PEOPLE. Ah—h-h-h-h!

[*They groan and weave their hands about in a tempest of sorrow and grieving.* DALE *steps swiftly off at the right to the place of execution. The organ gravely and sorrowfully reprises the "Chevy Chase" song, and the scene fades out. The light comes up on the incline at the left, showing* JONAS *standing there with his musket.*]

JONAS. [*Sorrowfully.*] With the killing of them pitiful poor fellows, the people learned their lesson to the bone. Aye, they did. And with their hearts beat down they went on with their work, no matter how bitter the thoughts that brewed inside 'em— And never a whiff of treason or rebellion in them any more. The power of the governor and his soldiers hung over them and there was naught else to do. And Master Rolfe hisself counseled patient endurance and long-suffering. Then when Captain Argall sailed in from England with his supplies of horses and cows and bullocks, goats, hogs and a whole swarm of poultry, our spirits were lifted up some and we begun to ease out of our sorrow. But Avis Webb could never find easement from hers for the murder of her husband. And one icy winter night she went out on the river there and drowned herself, and Barbara and me took her sweet little baby Charity to raise. [*Shaking his shoulders.*] Other settlements were started now—six in all. And Governor Dale said that with this wide spread of the people over the land his work was nighing an end and soon he would go back to England to the young wife that waited lonesome for him there. And the Indians seemed all at peace too, and Master Rolfe worked hard amongst them trying to bring 'em to Christianity. He started a Bible class here at the fort to teach 'em. But only one got r'ally converted, a quiet young fellow named Chanco. All the rest were pretending, as we later found out. For whilst them and old Opecancanough were coming and going in the fort and talking brotherhood and trading furs and skins for guns and hoes and axes, that scoundrelly chief was plotting our complete destruction. But Chanco stood true to the end and served the Rolfe household faithful like a dog.

So it was the spring of 1616 come on now, and Sir Thomas stood proud before the church ready to sail to England with twenty thousand pounds of good Virginia tobacco on his ship. And Master Rolfe and Pocahontas—nobody would ever call her Rebecca 'cepting her husband and Reverend Master Buck—they were set to sail with him. She had put aside the dark prophesying of her death and was bent on going to see the king and the great men at court to get help for her people—medicine and books and teachers, she said, for their uplifting. And Master Rolfe too was taking a petition from the colony to the Company and the king, signed by Captains Yeardley, Martin, Powell, West and the leaders, for getting of our rights and privileges so long promised unto us.

[*A trumpet blows a fanfare from the darkness of the center stage. The light fades from* JONAS *as he walks down the incline, and comes up on the center stage.*]

Scene IV

Interior of the fort. Some fifty or sixty of the colony are assembled in the marketplace, and DALE *with a document in his hand is standing on the upper level at the back beaming out at them.* SAVAGE *and* SPELMAN *are standing to the right of him blowing the trumpet and beating the drum respectively. Most of the men are puffing pipes.* ROLFE *and* POCAHONTAS *in their best finery are at the right center and with them the three Indian maids and an Indian youth,* CHANCO, *20, who carries little* THOMAS *in his arms.* OPECANCANOUGH *in his striking tribal dress and some six or eight of his men are over at the left.* BARBARA *at the right holds her adopted baby against her shoulder.* JONAS *comes in and stands by her, taking a joyous peep at the child as he does so. The scene is one of good spirits.* DALE *lifts the document he holds in his hand and the trumpet and drum grow silent.*

DALE. Now after these years of unremitting toil and difficulty, our task is completed. Ye founders of this enterprise have labored long and well and have endured unbelievable hardship to bring this colony to permanence and this day. For all this my thanks—the thanks of his majesty the king and of all England. I warrant some of ye have hated me and dreamed of murdering me in my bed. But you never did so. For this too my thanks.

[*A few of the people laugh.*]

You have hated the military rule by which I governed ye, I know. It was a rule of one for all, and none for himself—a true communism. And without it we never would have succeeded. Now you are sending by Master Rolfe a petition for your own representation, for your own voice in your own affairs. I tell you at this parting hour I shall give my voice to this petition back in England.

[*The people applaud spontaneously.*]

PEOPLE. Cheers for Governor Dale! Governor Dale! [DALE *bows.*]

DALE. But this martial law is not yet ended. It is the order of the Company that it continue with the deputy-governor till different orders be sent. And that new governor is to be one you have trusted long—him and his good lady—[*In announcement.*] Captain George Yeardley!

[*The cheering breaks out loudly, and a number of people rush up to* YEARDLEY *and shake his hand, congratulating him and* TEMPERANCE.]

PEOPLE. Captain Yeardley! Captain Yeardley! Mistress Temperance! Ray! ray!

[YEARDLEY *smiles about him and lifts his hand in recognition of their applause.* TEMPERANCE *takes his arm pridefully.*]

DALE. Yea, with him as leader Virginia will thrive—even as we are now thriving in these our six planted settlements—[*Enumerating joyously.*]—here at Jamestown the capital, 50 officers and laborers—at Henrico 38 officers and laborers—at Bermuda 119—at West and Shirley Hundred 25—at Kecoughtan 20—and at Dale's Gift near the coast 17—and besides all these in general 81 farmers and 65 women and children, boys and girls, in every place—amounting in all to 415 alive and strong—[*Soberly.*]—of the nearly three thousand who have come to dwell and labor here. [*Then more brightly as he looks at the document in his hands.*] And of the listing made by Master Rolfe there are in the colony 83 cows and heifers, 41 steers, 20 bulls, 3 horses, 3 mares, 216 goats and kids, and hogs running wild not to be numbered. And these last will multiply like the seed of Abraham. [*Holding up the paper.*] And now farewell to ye all and to the scenes of our trials and our triumphs. To you, Chief Opecancanough and your people, farewell. Ere another twelve months pass away Master Rolfe and his good lady will bring you good news and tokens of great aid from our king, our Company, and our English people. May you all continue in peace and harmony in the days ahead is my prayer. [*He steps forward and shakes* OPECANCANOUGH's *hand.*]

OPECANCANOUGH. [*With a deep bow and croaking out his words.*] Farewell, mighty werowance!

DALE. [*Lifting his hand.*] Farewell.

PEOPLE. Farewell.

[AUSTIN *pushes forward, leading* GOODY *out of the group to the left of the governor.*]

AUSTIN. A most special farewell, your honor, to me

and mine. [GOODY *is now revealed with two babies, one on each arm.* AUSTIN *gestures proudly to them and the people laugh and clap their hands.*] My two young sons, sir, twins. The oldest there, by half an hour, is named for thee—Thomas.

DALE. I am honored.

AUSTIN. And the younger there is—John.

DALE. I know—for John Rolfe.

AUSTIN. True, sir, for the both of ye who have done most for this settlement.

DALE. Felicitations on thy valor, Austin.

[*The people laugh.*]

AUSTIN. And now, your honor, that you be returning home to thy dear lady across the sea, this small parting gift, sir. [*He hands up a small packet to* DALE.]

DALE. [*Taking it.*] So?

AUSTIN. For thy using, sir—a goodly piece of Virginia snakeroot. [*He gestures toward the twins.*]

[*The men guffaw and the women giggle.* DALE, *grinning broadly, holds the packet up and looks at it.*]

DALE. [*Merrily.*] I doubt not in time this like tobacco will become a profitable commodity of English trade. And now, aboard! [*The trumpet and the drum sound again, and he leads the way out at the right rear.* POCAHONTAS *turns to* OPECANCANOUGH *to say goodbye, putting out both hands to him. He stares at her, making no move. She looks at him sorrowfully. Several of the* WARRIORS *now run over and bow low before her. Weeping, she tells them farewell.*]

POCAHONTAS. Anath.

WARRIORS. Anath.

[ROLFE *takes her arm, and they hurry away after the others, the three* MAIDS *and* CHANCO *following with little* THOMAS. *The scene fades out, and after a moment of darkness the light comes up on* JONAS *standing over on the left incline holding little* CHARITY *in his arms.*]

JONAS. Back in England the king and the people give Sir Thomas a mighty splurging of hooray-ing and hurrah-ing for what he had done here. And Pocahontas was mightily honored too and a power of things writ about her in broadsides and books and her pitcher painted by the court artist. And Lord Delaware and his lady and the high bishop hisself waited on her and took her before the king and queen, as 'twas told. And his majesty hearkened unto her and promised much help in tools and preachers and missionaries for her people. And great crowds followed her wherever she went. The Company and parliament likewise hearkened to our petition. Aye, it seemed all was bright ahead. And then our sad great loss was suffered to be remembered on that page of history Master Rolfe talks about. For in the cold dark English climate the sweet and gentle-hearted Pocahontas begun to sicken on down to death. He hurried her away on the good ship *George* home-returning, but too late. And there one night on the River Thames at the little town of Gravesend—of proper naming—the grieving ones waited by her bed.

[*He rises and starts quietly down the incline.* BARBARA *comes up to meet him and takes the baby. The light fades out and rises again over on the right side stage. The organ begins softly playing the lamentation hymn of the former burial scene.*]

Scene V

A sort of cubby hole sleeping nook aboard ship, with a square porthole showing at the rear. POCAHONTAS *is lying on a rude mattress, her head pillowed up, and the ship's* CAPTAIN *and the* SURGEON *are attending her. Two colonist women bound for Virginia are standing by. One of her Indian maids is seated on a box in the shadows, holding little* THOMAS *bundled up in her arms. He is now about two years old. The surgeon who is bending over* POCAHONTAS *straightens up and turns away. The organ continues its soft lament.*

SURGEON. The windy humors have now reached her vitals. She cannot endure the bleeding lancet again. [*To the* CAPTAIN.] You must let fall your anchor till morning, Captain.

[*The* CAPTAIN *makes an irritated gesture over the delay and goes out of the scene at the left.*]

WOMAN. So kind, so gentle she is. She never complains.

ROLFE. Soon, my darling, we shall be back in Virginia and you will mend there.

[POCAHONTAS *opens her eyes and smiles faintly at him.*]

POCAHONTAS. Our son—let him 'bide here safe till all is well.

[*She stretches out her arms, and the Indian maid brings little* THOMAS *over to her.* ROLFE *helps raise her up, and she kisses the child.*]

He is like thee—our son—his red hair, his eyes—[*Smiling.*]—his big hands.

ROLFE. Nay, like thee—

[*The maid lifts the child back into the shadows, and* POCAHONTAS *touches* ROLFE's *face as he kneels by her.*]

POCAHONTAS. The night—you remember—I say to you I bring you many strong sons—I'm a strong girl—and you say our children will grow brave and free—in the new land.

ROLFE. And they will.

POCAHONTAS. Our son will—in our Virginia—with the happy people there—my people, your people.

ROLFE. Yes.

POCAHONTAS. We believe so—we did work so.

ROLFE. Aye, suffered for that, and it shall be.

POCAHONTAS. And the great king promises much help. My people will read in the book—the blessed Bible—[*Her hands flutter about the coverlet for the Bible lying by.* ROLFE *gives it to her. She grasps it tightly, kisses it, and murmurs as she closes her eyes.*] It keep me safe. The Lord and his Book be my stony rock and my defense.

ROLFE. [*Prompting her.*] My strength and my redeemer.

POCAHONTAS. [*Answering.*] The Lord is my shepherd.

ROLFE. I shall not want.

POCAHONTAS. He maketh me to lie down in green pastures—

[ROLFE *joins in, and they both go on reciting in unison.*]

ROLFE AND POCAHONTAS. He leadeth me beside the still waters. He restoreth my soul. He leadeth me in the paths of righteousness for his name's sake.

[*Faraway an Indian drum begins to beat, growing louder and louder as* POCAHONTAS *hears it. Her voice dies out as she listens.* ROLFE *does not hear it and continues to recite the psalm.*]

ROLFE. Yea, though I walk through the valley of the shadow of death—I will fear no evil, for thou art with me. Thy rod and thy staff—

[POCAHONTAS *starts up with a scream.*]

POCAHONTAS. The drum! The drum! Opecancanough makes his bad medicine in the wilderness! Quick, quick! [*She tries to crawl off the mattress, shrieking.*] Mattah! Mattah!

[ROLFE *takes her in his arms as she struggles and screams.*]

Save the colony! Ireh assuminge! Ah—

[*Her head falls over and she lies limp in* ROLFE's *arms. The drum begins to fade away. The* CAPTAIN *re-enters.* ROLFE *broken-heartedly lays her back on the mattress.*]

ROLFE. [*With a sob.*] No, no! Pocahontas!

[*The* SURGEON *bends over her again, then gestures to the* CAPTAIN.]

SURGEON. She is at rest now, Master Rolfe.

ROLFE. It cannot be! [*With a wild raging cry.*] She's dead! Dead!

[*He bows over her sobbing. One of the women comes over and puts her hand comfortingly on his shoulder.*]

WOMAN. She's safe in Arthur's bosom to suffer no more. God's will be done, Master Rolfe.

ROLFE. Aye, aye. [*Gazing at* POCAHONTAS, *the tears pouring down his face.*] She gave her life away—gave it for the colony—for her people. Ah, we have killed her. [*Beating his hands together.*] Now all is dust and crumbling death in here. [*He strikes his breast a heavy blow.*] Help me, merciful Father, help me to bear this darkness! [*He bends over her.*] She was so sweet— [*Staring down at her.*]—so precious and so sweet!

[*He holds her lifeless form to him, kissing her quiet lips. The scene fades out, and the organ comes in again with a short reprise of its sorrowful lament. There is an instant of silence and darkness, and then the Indian war drum begins its wild beating again over in the woods of the left side stage. The light comes up there.*]

scene VI

A demonic war dance is under way in the forest. OPECANCANOUGH, *his son* KOCOUM, *and their warriors painted for battle, are dancing around their okie with yells and screeching song and the accompaniment of the pounding drum. A demented* RAWHUNT *is beating his gourd rattles in the air and keeping up a vibrating shuffle of frothy-mouthed fury and hate. Other warriors enter and join the dance, and all share in the wild boasting of the Indians' power against the white man.*

INDIANS. [*Led by* OPECANCANOUGH *and* KOCOUM.]
        Matanerew shashashewaw,
        Erawango peche coma,
        Whe whe yah hah hah,
        Nehe witowa, witowa!

[*They repeat their war chant over and over, brandishing their bows, muskets and a number of steel hatchets. In a concerted rush they spring toward a stump as the drum thunders away and drive their hatchets into it, sinking them as it were deep in the body of their enemy. Then they jerk them out and spring off into the darkness of the forest at the rear. The drum dies. The light fades out and comes up on the woodland side stage at the right.* JONAS *is standing there straight and stiff with his musket. He turns toward the audience.*]

JONAS. Aye and so it was that Opecancanough and his son Kocoum were rousing their people for a do-or-die massacre of the different settlements, though we didn't learn about it till it was too late. Opecancanough was lord and chief of all the tribes with two thousand warriors now. The aged Powhatan had died, some said of a broken heart over the death of his daughter Pocahontas and the pushing of his people back before the spreading colony, and his brother ruled in his stead. And there at Jamestown our beloved governor, now Sir George Yeardley, and his lady with him, were standing before the people happy and jubilant over the good news out of England, and the burgesses had gathered there happy with them— And not a solitary soul was dreaming of the storm of hate about to break upon their heads.

[*The light fades out as* JONAS *goes down the incline and comes up on the center stage. A trumpet and drum begin to sound.*]

Scene VII

The interior of the fort, with the church and cabin and court of guard building arranged as in the early part of the play. The joyous COLONISTS *are assembled there, fifty or sixty of them, including many of our old acquaintances, men and woman, and the new group of burgesses.* JOHN ROLFE *is standing with* YEARDLEY *and* TEMPERANCE *on the upper level with a record book in his hand.* BUCK *is behind them with his Bible. Over at the right* SAVAGE *is blowing his trumpet and* SPELMAN *is beating his drum. When the light comes up the people are mixing their cheering in with the martial sounds,* AUSTIN *being one of the most vociferous.*

VOICES. [*With* AUSTIN *leading the way.*] Cheers for our governor—Sir George Yeardley. 'Ray, 'ray!

OTHER VOICES. Cheers for Lady Yeardley! 'Ray!

[YEARDLEY *holds up his hand, his face wreathed in smiles. The trumpet and drum die.*]

YEARDLEY. At this hour we give devout thanks unto God for his infinite mercy. For now with our new charter we are confirmed in those rights and privileges we have labored so long to win.

VOICES. Hear, hear!

YEARDLEY. And we honor our friend John Rolfe for his service therein, who is now declared to be the secretary and recorder of this colony.

VOICES. Aye, aye! We do. Blessings on John Rolfe.

YEARDLEY. And his long grief is our grief, his loss our loss. And no day passes, no hour even, that we do not hold in loving remembrance his young wife—our dear Pocahontas—who sleeps there beyond the sea, far from this settlement she loved and for which she gave her gentle life. In the symbol of her sacrifice the old land and the new are the more securely bound in their heartstrings.

VOICES. Yes, yes.

YEARDLEY. We have founded here in Virginia a new government, a representative government—the first in the new world—with duly elected burgesses—and we now pass our own laws, assess taxes, give title and deed to private property, and take any and all steps whatsoever as we see fit for our rights and needs. We must without stint conduct ourselves in justice and equity as becomes free men. The example we are setting here will be measured by generations that come after us. Call the roll, and the burgesses will assemble for the meeting in the church.

ROLFE. [*Reading from the book.*] For James City elected are—Captain William Powell and Ensign William Spence—[*As* ROLFE *reads the names, the* BURGESSES *step forward and stand in front of* YEARDLEY.] For the city of Henrico—Thomas Dowse and John Polentine. For Charles City—Samuel Sharpe and Samuel Jordan. For Kecoughtan—William Tucker and William Capp—

THE FOUNDERS

[*Suddenly the organ gives a loud alarm cry, and* CHANCO *comes tearing down the right incline and into the scene. He is spent from his hard exertions and stumbles and falls forward on his knees.*]

CHANCO. [*Gasping as* ROLFE *runs down and helps him to his feet.*] The Indians—Opecancanough—they march to Jamestown—they kill—they burn the plantations there! [*He gestures behind him.* YEARDLEY *calls out.*]

YEARDLEY. Where are they, Chanco?

ROLFE. He comes from my plantation across the river.

CHANCO. I come in boat to tell you. They murder the women and children—all. Quick! Help! Help!

YEARDLEY [*Yelling.*] Sound the alarum—let the soldiers be ready to march at once!

[*The scene is in a turmoil, and the women and children begin hurrying away to their different quarters as* SAVAGE *sounds the alarm on his trumpet and* SPELMAN *beats the drum.* BUCK *goes along comforting the women.*]

MARTIN. We must get help to the plantations!

POWELL. Prime the cannons!

[*Soldiers are hurrying across the scene from right to left, and some of them run up the walkway to stand on guard. The scene blacks out and then off in the woods at the left and right, above the woodland side stages, the Indian attack is revealed—representing the massacre on the plantations. Flashes of gunfire are seen in the woods followed by yells and shrieks, and we see a number of colonists rushing through the woods as they are pursued by the Indians. The organ mixes its turmoiling anguish in with the attack. The massacre continues on both sides of the amphitheatre, coming out on the side stages and then moving down toward the center stage —a number of Indians rushing on and into the fort. Other Indians are seen entering from the right and left of the market place, and some come climbing up over the palisades at the rear. There is a loud flash of flame, and a heavy explosion follows as the cannon are fired off. We see* YEARDLEY, POWELL, MARTIN, WEST, ROLFE, DODS, AUSTIN, READ, LAYDON, BARRET, SAVAGE, SPELMAN, *and others, now in hand-to-hand combat with the Indians—there at the rear of the stage and around the church and at the right and left. Up on the walkway some of the men are clubbing the attackers back. In the sound track a medley of whistling bullets and swishing arrows is heard. A few flaming arrows are shot into the thatch of the church and the court of guard building. Fires break out there and men hurry to extinguish them. Soldiers run in at the left and the right. The Indians are finally driven away toward the right.* OPECANCANOUGH *and* KOCOUM *come dashing in at the left, leading some of their warriors. The fighting continues. A number of colonists and Indians have been killed by this time—some sprawling awkwardly on the earth or half-hanging from the walkway, and here and there we see one trying to raise himself up, then slumping to the ground again and toppling over in the spasm of death. The screaming of the women is heard from different directions of the fort.* OPECANCANOUGH *and his men are driven now up the left incline. Other colonists fly to the right to defend the gates. We see* LAYDON *wounded and falling near the front of the scene.* ROLFE *runs over to help him. As he bends to lift him up,* KOCOUM *rushes back down the right incline. His face*

THE FOUNDERS

is streaked with blood. He springs on ROLFE *and stabs him.* ROLFE *falls.* KOCOUM *escapes up and into the woods. The sounds of the fighting begin to die away.* OPECANCANOUGH *appears for an instant out of the forest at the left.* LAYDON *raises his musket from where he is lying and shoots him. In the spotlight we see the chief as he flings up his arms with a yell, spins about and collapses to the ground.* DODS, BARRET *and* READ *run down out of the forest from the left with their muskets. They stop by the wounded chief.*]

DODS. 'Tis Opecancanough!

THE THREE. [*Yelling.*] Opecancanough!

[*They seize* OPECANCANOUGH *and drag him down the incline. A cheer goes up from the colonists from different directions. The smoke of battle which has been billowing over the scene is now clearing a bit.* YEARDLEY *and others are gathering in the center of the scene about the figure of* ROLFE.]

YEARDLEY. [*On his knees.*] Master John Rolfe is dead! [*The men take off their hats and crowd forward. The women begin entering again. The organ thunders in as the scene blacks out. There is an instant of darkness, and then the light is up once more. The colonists are gathered in front of* YEARDLEY. *The wounded and the dead have been removed.* YEARDLEY'S *voice sounds forth strong and exultant, as the organ dies down.*] Opecancanough is taken, his people scattered forever! At last this colony is safe. And all honor to those who gave their lives.

VOICES. [Loudly, solemnly.] Aye, blessed be their name.

YEARDLEY. Let us with one accord gather in the church and there give thanks to God for this great salvation. And with our tears and our words pay proper tribute to Master Rolfe and all the valiant dead.

[*He turns and leads the way up toward the church with* BUCK *and* TEMPERANCE *walking with him. The organ comes in with the "Huguenot Battle Hymn" with which the play opened and then softens down a bit as* JONAS *comes out at the right front.*]

JONAS. [*Vibrantly and swiftly.*] And so it was we settled Jamestown and founded our new nation in the world!

[*The organ surges in again and the scene fades out. After a moment of darkness the lights come up in the amphitheatre.*]

THE END

1. COLONIST LANDING HYMN

From the ancient "Huguenot Battle Hymn"

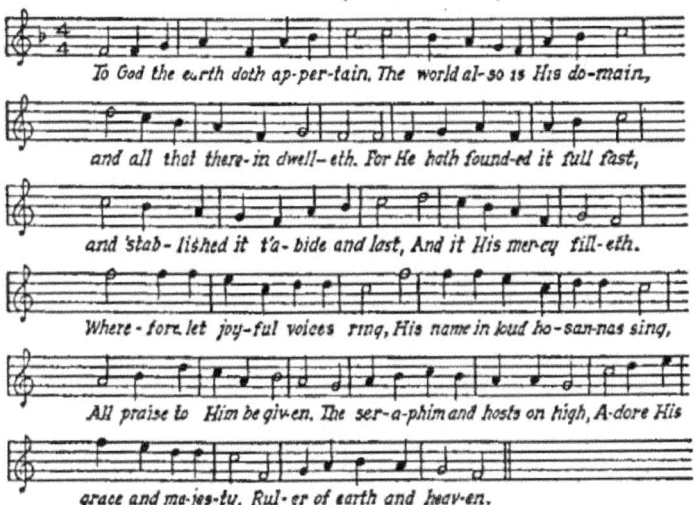

To God the earth doth ap-per-tain, The world al-so is His do-main, and all that there-in dwell-eth. For He hath found-ed it full fast, and 'stab-lished it t'a-bide and last, And it His mer-cy fill-eth. Where-fore let joy-ful voices ring, His name in loud ho-san-nas sing, All praise to Him be giv-en. The ser-a-phim and hosts on high, A-dore His grace and ma-jes-ty, Rul-er of earth and heav-en.

> Blessed is he whose filthy stain
> The Lord with pardon doth make clean,
>   Whose fault well-hidden lieth.
> Blessed indeed to whom the Lord
> Imputes not sins to be abhorred,
>   Whose spirit falsehood flieth.
> Thus I pressed down with weight of pain,
> Whether I silent did remain,
>   Or roared, my bones still wasted.
> For so both day and night did stand
> On wretched me thy heavy hand,
>   My life hot torments tasted,

2. SALUTE TO THE LAND

3. ALARM CALL

4. COLONIST WORK SONG
From E. Johnson

Heave ho, ye men of Eng-land, stout of heart and hand,
We toil for God and king and thus sub-due the land. Fast
in the wild-er-ness we build our hearth and home, Far
o-ver oc-ean's might-y main and salt-sea foam. -- Through
heat and rain and cold we car-ry on, to cease not till
this bless-ed work be done.

'Twas in the merry month of May we landed here --
To work, to work, the captain said in accents clear,
With axe and adze and hoe, the hammer and the maul,
Yea, swing them with a right good will and let them fall !
   --Through heat and rain and cold we carry on,
     To cease not till this blessed work be done.

5. INDIAN SONG FOR JOHN SMITH

6. AUSTIN COOMS' SONG
An old English ballad

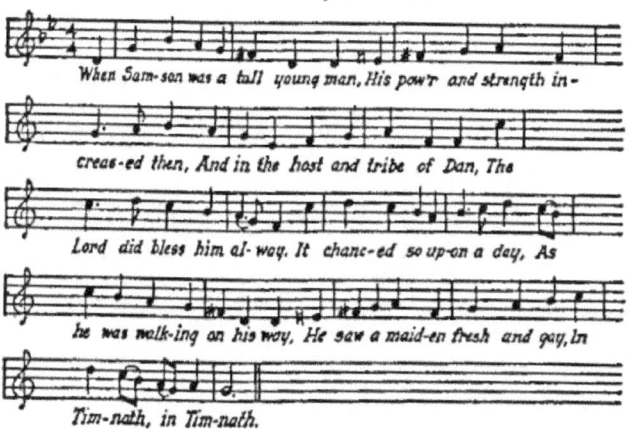

When Sam-son was a tall young man, His pow'r and strength in-creas-ed then, And in the host and tribe of Dan, The Lord did bless him al-way. It chanc-ed so up-on a day, As he was walk-ing on his way, He saw a maid-en fresh and gay, In Tim-nath, in Tim-nath.

With whom he fell so sore in love
That he his fancy could not move.
His parents therefore did he prove
    And craved their good wills.
I have found out a wife, quoth he,
I pray you, father, give her me,
Though she a stranger's daughter be,
    I passe not, I passe not.

Then on Delilah fair and bright
Did Samson set his whole delight,
Whom he did love both day and night
    Which wrought his overthrow.
For she with sweet words did intreat
That for her sake he would repeat
Wherein his strength that was so great
    Consisted, consisted.

7. COLONIST FUNERAL HYMN
From G. Kirby

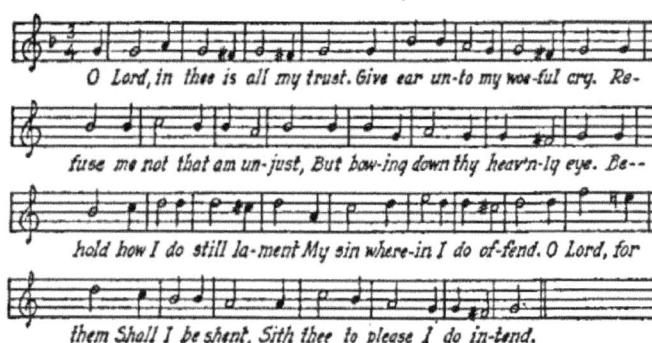

O Lord, in thee is all my trust. Give ear un-to my woe-ful cry. Re-fuse me not that am un-just, But bow-ing down thy heav'n-ly eye. Be-hold how I do still la-ment My sin where-in I do of-fend. O Lord, for them Shall I be shent, Sith thee to please I do in-tend.

O God, my God, wherefore dost thou
  In darkness leave me utterly,
And hear'st me not whilst I avow
  My ruin complete and misery?
To thee, my God, e'en all day long
  I raise my piteous plea and call..
O ease me of my woeful wrong
  And cleanse my heart of bitter gall!

8. COLONIST HYMN IN TIME OF STORM
From Edmund Hooper

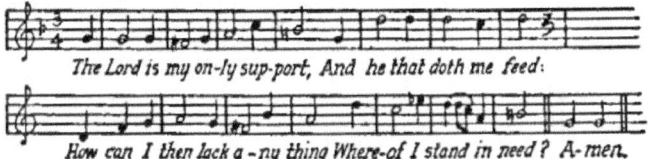

The Lord is my on-ly sup-port, And he that doth me feed: How can I then lack a-ny thing Where-of I stand in need? A-men.

2. He doth me fold in cotes most safe,
    The tender grass fast by:
    And after drives me to the streams
    Which run most pleasantly.

3. And when I feel myself near lost
    Then doth he home me take:
    Conducting me in his right paths
    E'en for his own name's sake.

4. And though I were e'en at death's door,
    Yet would I feel no ill:
    For by thy rod and shepherd's crook
    I am comforted still.

6. And finally, while breath doth last,
    Thy grace shall me defend:
    And in the house of God will I
    My life forever spend. Amen.

9. WATCHMAN'S CALL

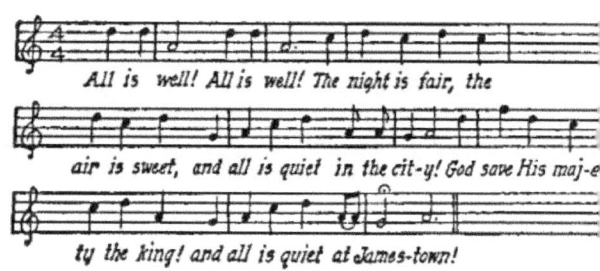

All is well! All is well! The night is fair, the air is sweet, and all is quiet in the cit-y! God save His maj-es-ty the king! and all is quiet at James-town!

10. JOHN ROLFE'S MARCHING SONG
Old English drinking song

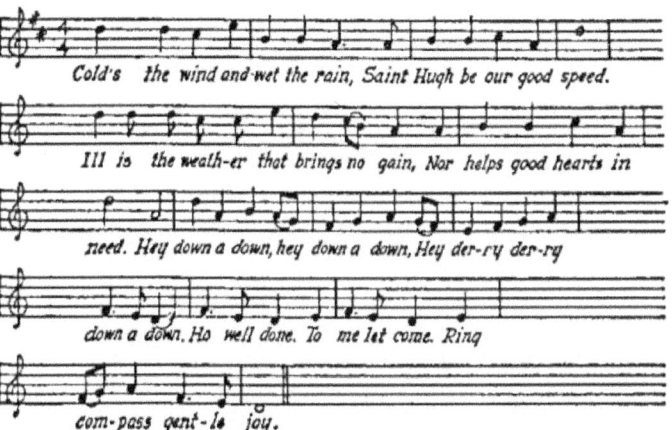

Cold's the wind and wet the rain, Saint Hugh be our good speed.
Ill is the weather that brings no gain, Nor helps good hearts in
need. Hey down a down, hey down a down, Hey der-ry der-ry
down a down. Ho well done. To me let come. Ring
com-pass gent-le joy.

> Troll the bowl, the jolly nutbrown bowl,
> And here, kind mate, to thee!
> Let's sing a dirge for Saint Hugh's soul
> And down it merrily.
> Hey down a down, etc.

11. ASSEMBLY CALL

12. THE LOWERING OF THE JAMESTOWN FLAG
Essex's Lamentation

13. MARTHA RAYNOR'S SONG
Old English folksong

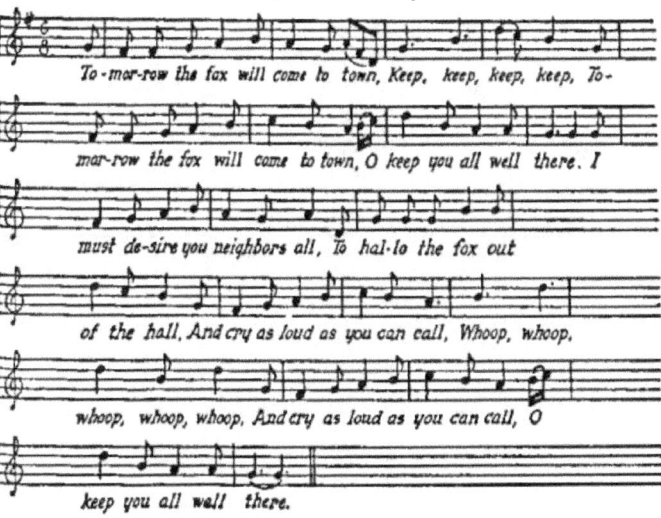

To-mor-row the fox will come to town, Keep, keep, keep, keep, To-mar-row the fox will come to town, O keep you all well there. I must de-sire you neighbors all, To hal-lo the fox out of the hall, And cry as loud as you can call, Whoop, whoop, whoop, whoop, whoop, And cry as loud as you can call, O keep you all well there.

He'll steal the cock out from the flock .....

He'll steal the hen out of the pen .....

He'll steal the duck out of the brook .....

He'll steal the lamb e'en from his dam .....

14. POCAHONTAS' LAMENT FOR THE COLONY

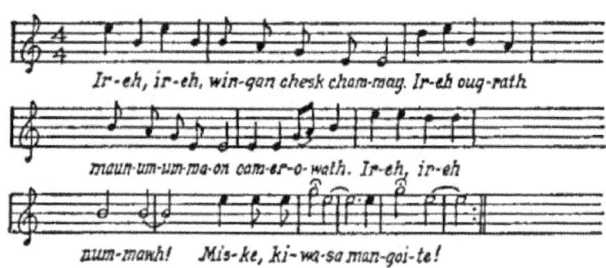

15. GOVERNOR DALE'S FOLKSONG
Old English Folksong

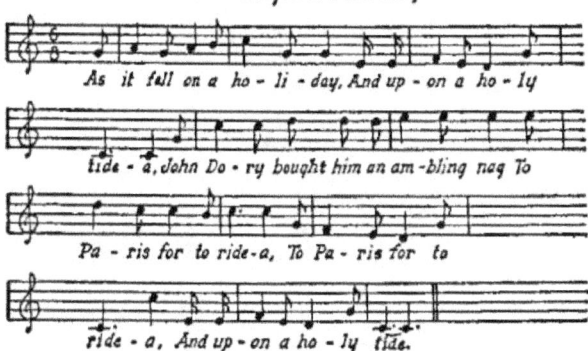

As it fell on a ho-li-day, And up-on a ho-ly tide-a, John Do-ry bought him an am-bling nag To Pa-ris for to ride-a, To Pa-ris for to ride-a, And up-on a ho-ly tide.

The first man that John Dory did meet,
Was good King John of France-a:
John Dory could well of his courtesie,
But fell down in a france-a.

The roaring cannons then were plied,
And dub-a-dub went the drum-a;
The braying trumpets loud they cried,
To courage both all and some-a.

16. JAMESTOWN MAIDS' FOLKSONG
Old English folksong

Sum-mer is a-com-ing in, Loud-ly sing cuck-oo!
Grow-eth seed and blow-eth mead, And spring-eth the wood now.
Sing cuck-oo! Ew-e bleat-eth aft-er lamb, Low'th aft-er calf the cow. Bul-lock start-eth, Buck to fern go'th,
Mer-ry sing cuck-oo, cuck-oo, cuck-oo. Well sing'st thou cuc-oo-- Nor cease thou nev-er now.

17. THE WEDDING OF POCAHONTAS -- PROCESSIONAL HYMN
From J. Farmer

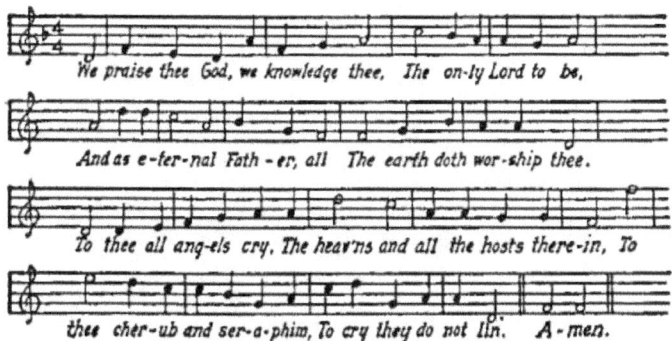

We praise thee God, we knowledge thee, The on-ly Lord to be,
And as e-ter-nal Fath-er, all The earth doth wor-ship thee.
To thee all ang-els cry, The heav'ns and all the hosts there-in, To
thee cher-ub and ser-a-phim, To cry they do not lin. A-men.

Exalt your heads, ye gates on high,
Ye doors that last for ay.
Be lift, for now our Lord and king
Doth through you make his way.
Who is this glorious king, I say?
The Lord of hosts most high,
E'n he that rules the earth and sea
In pow'r and majesty!

18. MADRIGAL FOR THE WEDDING OF POCAHONTAS
From Thomas Morley

19. COLONIST DANCE AT THE WEDDING OF POCAHONTAS
From Thomas Morley

20. THE CONSPIRATORS' FOLK-BALLAD
Ancient English ballad

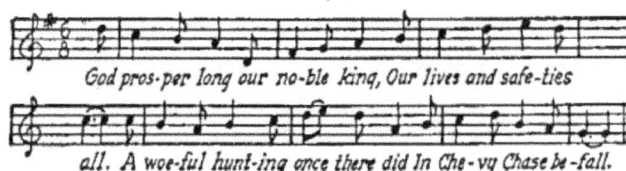

God pros-per long our no-ble king, Our lives and safe-ties all. A woe-ful hunt-ing once there did In Che-vy Chase be-fall.

To drive the deer with hound and horn
　Earl Percy took his way.
The child may rue that is unborn
　The hunting of that day.

Earl Douglas on his milk-white steed,
　Most like a baron bold,
Rode foremost of his company
　Whose armor shone like gold.

Our English archers bent their bows,
　Their hearts were good and true,
At the first flight of arrows sent,
　Full four-score Scots they slew.

They closed full fast on every side,
　No slackness there was found,
And many a gallant gentleman
　Lay gasping on the ground.

O Christ! it was a grief to see,
　And likewise for to hear
The cries of men lying in their gore,
　And scattered here and there.

21. GOODY COOMS' WASHTUB SONG
Old English folksong

There was a jo-vial tin-ker, Who was a good ale drink-er, He ne-ver was a shrink-er, Be-lieve me this is true. And he came from the Weald of Kent, When all his mon-ey was gone and spent, Which made him look like a Jack-a-lent. And Joan's ale is new, And Joan's ale is new, my boys, And Joan's ale is new.

The tinker he did settle
Most like a man of mettle,
And vow'd to pawn his kettle;
Now mark what did ensue;
His neighbors they flock in apace,
To see Tom Tinker's comely face,
Where they drank soundly for a space,
Whilst Joan's ale, etc. etc.

22. THE YOUNG MOTHERS' FOLK BALLAD
Old English ballad

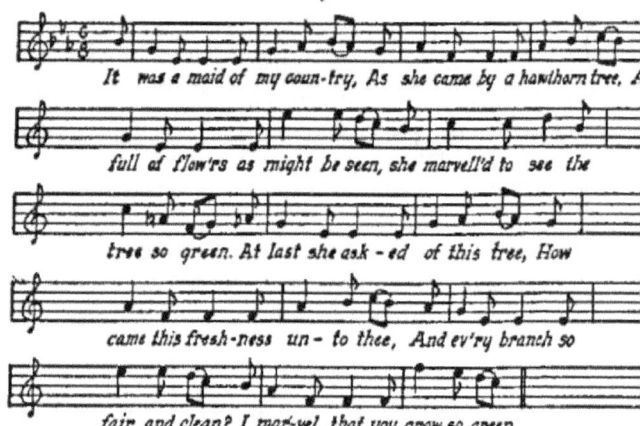

It was a maid of my coun-try, As she came by a hawthorn tree, A full of flow'rs as might be seen, she marvell'd to see the tree so green. At last she ask-ed of this tree, How came this fresh-ness un- to thee, And ev'ry branch so fair and clean? I mar-vel that you grow so green.

The tree made answer by and by,
I have cause to grow triumphantly,
The sweetest dew that ever be seen
Doth fall on me to keep me green.

23. JAMESTOW LULLABY
Ancient English carol

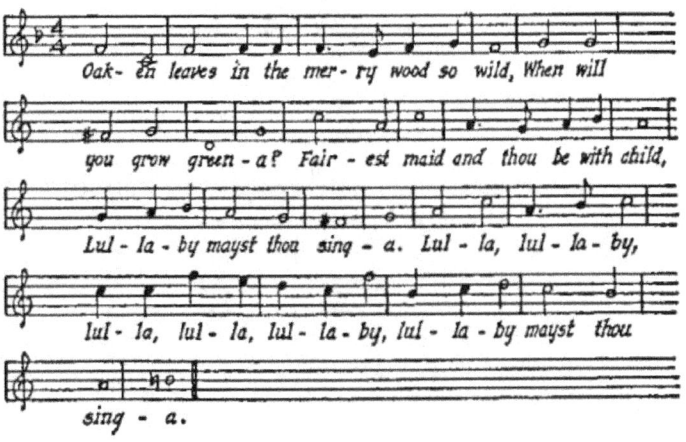

Oak-en leaves in the mer-ry wood so wild, When will you grow green-a? Fair-est maid and thou be with child, Lul-la-by mayst thou sing-a. Lul-la, lul-la-by, lul-la, lul-la, lul-la-by, lul-la-by mayst thou sing-a.

24. OPECANCANOUGH'S WAR SONG

Mat - a - ne - rew sha - sha - she - waw,
Er - a - wan - go, pech - e com - a, Whe whe yah hah
hah, Ne - he wit - o - wa! wit - o - wa!
Mat - a - ne - rew sha - sha - she - waw,
Er - a - wan - go pech - e com - a! Hah! Hah!

25. THE MASSACRE ALARM CALL

No one shall make any changes in this title(s) for the purpose of production. No part of this book may be reproduced, stored in a retrieval system, scanned, uploaded, or transmitted in any form, by any means, now known or yet to be invented, including mechanical, electronic, digital, photocopying, recording, videotaping, or otherwise, without the prior written permission of the publisher. No one shall share this title(s), or any part of this title(s), through any social media or file hosting websites.

For all inquiries regarding motion picture, television, online/digital and other media rights, please contact Concord Theatricals Corp.

MUSIC AND THIRD PARTY MATERIALS USE NOTE

Licensees are solely responsible for obtaining formal written permission from copyright owners to use copyrighted music and/or other copyrighted third-party materials (e.g., artworks, logos) in the performance of this play and are strongly cautioned to do so. If no such permission is obtained by the licensee, then the licensee must use only original music and materials that the licensee owns and controls. Licensees are solely responsible and liable for clearances of all third-party copyrighted materials, including without limitation music, and shall indemnify the copyright owners of the play(s) and their licensing agent, Concord Theatricals Corp., against any costs, expenses, losses and liabilities arising from the use of such copyrighted third-party materials by licensees. For music, please contact the appropriate music licensing authority in your territory for the rights to any incidental music.

IMPORTANT BILLING AND CREDIT REQUIREMENTS

If you have obtained performance rights to this title, please refer to your licensing agreement for important billing and credit requirements.

www.ingramcontent.com/pod-product-compliance
Lightning Source LLC
Chambersburg PA
CBHW072000290426
44109CB00018B/2085